Lear's
Self-Discovery

LEAR'S SELF-DISCOVERY

by

Paul A. Jorgensen

UNIVERSITY OF CALIFORNIA PRESS
BERKELEY AND LOS ANGELES

1967

UNIVERSITY OF CALIFORNIA PRESS
BERKELEY AND LOS ANGELES, CALIFORNIA

CAMBRIDGE UNIVERSITY PRESS
LONDON, ENGLAND

© 1967 BY THE REGENTS OF THE UNIVERSITY OF CALIFORNIA

LIBRARY OF CONGRESS CATALOG CARD NUMBER: 67-10462

DESIGNED BY PAMELA F. JOHNSON

PRINTED IN THE UNITED STATES OF AMERICA

To
my mother and the memory of my father

Acknowledgments

The student who for many years moves about in the bleak, troubled solitude of the *King Lear* terrain is, sometimes reassuringly, sometimes annoyingly, aware that he is not entirely alone. There are always human voices—instructive, admonitory, possessive—of fellow students; so that the experience of sitting down to reread the play is not quite the agonizingly private and fresh one that it was for Samuel Johnson and John Keats.

Nevertheless, there is a quality about the play which, I believe, sets it apart from Shakespeare's other tragedies. It seems to demand more, and intimately more, from the reader than any other. That is one reason for believing that the theme of self-discovery in the play is so central. It is not only Lear but the reader who, ultimately in solitude, must burn through

the fierce dispute
Betwixt damnation and impassion'd clay,

exposing himself to situations that make him, like Lear, question his very identity and—what is finally the same thing—the nature of "impassion'd clay."

It is not, therefore, out of a feeling of self-sufficiency that I must claim, when considering my indebtedness to others, that, like most books on *King Lear*, this is largely a personal interpretation, given whatever objectivity and steadiness it possesses by reference to a body of Renaissance books on self-knowledge. I only hope that the self-discovery does not prove to be primarily that of the author himself.

But though the responsibility for the book must be basically mine, and though many to whom I wish to acknowledge indebtedness might prefer it to remain that way, certain kinds of help simply must be acknowledged. Joan Ancell, whose services were made available to me through a UCLA research grant, has proved to be a discerning and dependable assistant and typist, and to her I am also grateful for help with the index. To my student Julian Rice, my research assistant from the UCLA Center for Medieval and Renaissance Studies, I am similarly indebted for intelligent help. Both of these students, through their interest in the project, greatly expedited the terminal stages of my work.

William Elton's book *King Lear and the Gods* (San Marino, Calif.: The Huntington Library, 1966) had not appeared when this volume went to press. Although I regret not having been able to make use of it, I did have several opportunities to discuss my subject with Professor Elton and I benefited from his seminar on *King Lear* at the Huntington Library. He is of course in no way responsible for my point of view.

Rolf Soellner, who is completing a larger study of self-knowledge in Shakespeare's plays, has generously and helpfully corresponded with me about his project. Professor Soellner's book will, I am sure, be a more adequate treatment of a very large subject than is my exploratory essay on one play.

My colleagues Ralph Cohen and Blake Nevius have, through encouraging and stimulating conversation, and most of all through friendship, made my task much more pleasant.

Finally, I must acknowledge, as I have in the past, my obligations to the Huntington Library and to its helpful staff, notably John M. Steadman and Mary Isabel Fry. Most of the rare books to which I refer in the second chapter were consulted at that exemplary institution. In fact, they were so readily and attractively available there that I may have slipped into thinking that they were at one time far more delightful and important than they actually were.

P. A. J.

Contents

After a little I am taken in and put to bed. Sleep, soft smiling, draws me unto her: and those receive me, as one familiar and well-beloved in that home: but will not, oh, will not, not now, not ever; but will not ever tell me who I am.

—JAMES AGEE
"Knoxville: Summer 1915"
from A Death in the Family, 1957

I
Introduction

The subject of the present study is a cliché. But like all clichés it needs reexamination once it has reached the point where it not only is no longer valuable but has become a menace and a nuisance, both to literary criticism and to teaching. I am attempting, therefore, a rather full, and I hope fresh, study of Lear's self-discovery, its intellectual meaning, and its dramatic expression. I shall try to show, in small part, what self-knowledge meant to Shakespeare's contemporaries and, most important, how he struck out on his own, and with insights well beyond his time, to create perhaps the greatest drama of self-discovery in all literature. I choose for the title "self-discovery" rather than "self-knowledge" because it is closer to the dynamic quality of the dramatic experience. Self-knowledge is the *content* of what, if I am right, Lear attains; self-discovery is the intellectual and dramatic process whereby he attains it. But it is necessary to consider both.

That *King Lear* is a play much concerned with the need for and the process of self-discovery is suggested by many of its lines. Most important are Regan's coldly intelligent analysis of her father's irrational behavior, "yet he hath ever but slenderly known himself" (I.i.296–297), and Lear's grand question—perhaps the most important one in literature, if not in life—"Who is it that can tell me who I am?" (I.iv.250).[1] A few friends and enemies can help to tell him, but he must fundamentally learn for himself. "I would learn that," he continues—sarcastically at this point, and with the dramatic irony that he does not understand the full requirements of the curriculum in which he is enrolling. Further evidence that the play is much concerned with self-discovery is, of course, the fact that many critics, principally recent ones, have found it to be so and have by scattered and generally brief comments come to

[1] All Shakespearean quotations are taken from *The Complete Plays and Poems of William Shakespeare*, ed. by William Allan Neilson and Charles Jarvis Hill (Cambridge, Mass.: Houghton Mifflin Company, 1942).

accept it as a cliché of *King Lear* criticism. This is not to say that
the comments have not been diverse; in some respects they have
been confusingly so. But they are also massively unified, I think, in
the conclusions that are least important or most likely to be mistaken. In our attempt to break up what is stereotyped, without
forfeiting the benefits of the superior and less regimented insights,
we shall look at some of the better approaches presently.

If *King Lear* is the ultimate drama of self-discovery, this may
help to explain why it is also perhaps the most totally compelling
of all Shakespeare's plays. Whatever we may have to say about the
depth of the experience of self-recognition—and psychologists will
confirm that it is a shattering one—we must not forget that in a
play it is also a dramatic experience. Though it is not precisely
what Aristotle meant by anagnorisis, and though Shakespeare may
not have been well aquainted with the *Poetics*, Aristotle was brilliantly describing one of the immutable laws of great tragedy when
he listed recognition or discovery as one of its essentials. A modern
instance will illustrate the fact that though one is not thinking of
Aristotle, one cannot avoid him. Archibald MacLeish did not have
Aristotle in mind when he wrote *J. B.* In the trial run at Washington, D.C., the play came off fairly well, but something was lacking
to bring it to a true conclusion and satisfy the audience. Without
at first thinking about Aristotle (whom he knew only too well but
had not thought it necessary to consult for a modern play), Mac-
Leish in a moment of "independent" insight realized that he
needed a recognition or discovery scene. He supplied it, and the
play was a success, as well as a respectable example of tragic art.

By anagnorisis Aristotle did not apparently have in mind quite
the psychological experience that critics have found in *King Lear*.
For Aristotle, the term was best exemplified by Oedipus, who discovered that he was the son of Laius and that his wife was really
his mother. The question of identity was not one of inner character, but of who, in terms of family relationship and name, was
who. Such a disclosure does not lead, in a modern sense, to the
fullest of self-understanding. It is a matter of physical rather than
psychological identity. True, there is much of psychological self-
awareness in Sophocles' play. But Aristotle was describing Greek
tragedy as a whole, and in it mistaken identity is primarily the con-

fusing of one person with another. It is not the confusing of what one thinks he is with what he truly is. Nevertheless, the dramatic principle involved is right and profound. An audience does not experience the fullest of tragic pleasure unless the protagonist recognizes what the audience sees is wrong in his view of himself and of life. If a protagonist is struck down in ignorance, we have not tragedy but what Robert B. Heilman has called the drama of disaster.[2] Bertrand Evans has shown that the Friar's long speech at the end of *Romeo and Juliet*, often cut in productions because the audience already knows everything that the Friar says, is no slip in dramaturgy on Shakespeare's part. Though the audience already knows what the actors do not know, the audience is intolerably ill at ease until it sees each member of the cast learn how ironically ignorant he has been of his role in the tragedy. This is precisely the self-illumination that Friar Laurence provides.[3] It is, then, the audience that requires the recognition. If it does not receive it, it experiences the frustration of watching an Iago refuse to talk, refuse to acknowledge how wrong he has been, as opposed to the aesthetically fulfilling experience of an Angelo, a Claudius, a Macbeth, or an Antony at least partially acknowledging his own nature and errors.

Thus anagnorisis, especially when combined with peripeteia, is an essential of the greatest tragedy, and we must not forget this dramatic aspect of self-discovery as we examine its intellectual qualities. But *King Lear* is, as Maynard Mack has remarked, "a problem," [4] and we shall not find the kind of explicit acknowledgment of error or identity which will fully satisfy an audience or comfort a single-minded critic. A part of Lear's recognition lies in generalized statements about man patterned on Renaissance require-

---

[2] *Shakespearian Tragedy and the Drama of Disaster,* Sedgewick Memorial Lecture, no. 3 (Vancouver: British Columbia University Press, 1960).

[3] "The Brevity of Friar Laurence," *PMLA,* LXV (1950), 841–865. Professor Evans' pioneering approach, making use of imperfect and discrepant awarenesses in the characters, has recently been searchingly applied to Shakespeare's comedies. See his *Shakespeare's Comedies* (Oxford: Clarendon Press, 1960).

[4] *King Lear in Our Time* (Berkeley and Los Angeles: University of California Press, 1965), p. 3. It was my misfortune that Professor Mack's perceptive and informative book did not reach me until I had completed the first draft of this study; and I have not, I fear, been able to make worthy use of it.

ments of self-discovery. Another part, examined in the fifth chapter, is concerned with Lear's quest for his own identity, and many of the verbal responses to this quest come from others as well as himself. But both approaches to self-discovery, one old and the other "modern," would be dramatically helpless without the Aristotelian concept of which Shakespeare may never have heard.

II

Only one critic—such is the inhibiting force of a stereotype—has devoted an article specifically to the subject of self-knowledge in *King Lear*. In "The Socratic Imperative and King Lear," [5] an article of only some eight pages, Raymond Jenkins traces the imperative of "know thyself," inscribed on the wall of the temple at Delphi, to several utterances of Socrates, though he admits that it may also be ascribed to any of six other Greek philosophers.[6] To Socrates, self-examination necessitated the examination of others, just as it in turn led to the knowledge of others (Xenophon's *Memorabilia*). There is, however, only slight apparent use of the Greek background in Jenkins' generalizations about what "know thyself" meant to Shakespeare. The fullest summary of his position is as follows:

To Shakespeare self-knowledge connoted self-control or temperance in all things, patience, and humility. To us, and doubtless to Shakespeare, self-knowledge implies the wisdom essential to right conduct, the ability to distinguish, as Socrates says, "between what one can do and what one cannot do," and hence "obtain what is good and guard against what is evil."

(p. 86)

This is applied specifically to Regan's "yet he hath ever but slenderly known himself" as stressing mainly "Lear's violent

---

[5] *Renaissance Papers 1963* (Southeastern Renaissance Conference, 1964), pp. 85–93.

[6] For a general study, see Eliza Gregory Wilkins, *The Delphic Maxims in Literature* (Chicago: University of Chicago Press, 1929).

temper and his lack of self-control, or patience." Jenkins' critera are not detailed enough to cover the complex pattern of self-discovery in *King Lear*. Far more than "right conduct" is involved and, though this is relevant, far more than control of a violent temper. Jenkins could have found more specific help in Shakespeare's own age than in Socrates. The Renaissance knew Socrates, and many of the treatises on self-knowledge owe something to him. But, in general, *nosce teipsum* meant a good deal more than what Jenkins said it did. Nevertheless, Jenkins makes some good critical observations about *King Lear*, notably the following:

> *Lear's plan of setting his rest on the "kind nursery" of his joy, Cordelia, was not unwise. If he had lived with Cordelia during his few remaining years, Lear would have received all the honor, love, and veneration due to an aged king. But he would never have acquired self-knowledge.*
>
> (p. 87)

Probably only those critics who believe that self-knowledge is essential to Lear's "redemption" would disagree with the first sentence of this quotation. It may well have been the "unwise" decision that saved Lear, in the fullest sense.

Besides substantial references to Lear's learning in *This Great Stage: Image and Structure in King Lear* (1948), Robert B. Heilman devotes a small, but compact, part of an article to the subject of self-knowledge in *King Lear* in " 'Twere Best not Know Myself: Othello, Lear, Macbeth." [7] This article is one of a series dealing with self-knowledge in the tragedies and having as their end what is emerging as a fresh view of the tragic. These are important studies; they are searching and flexible. Heilman studies failure as well as success in self-knowledge, and its dramatic implications. If I interpret his approach correctly, Heilman takes self-knowledge in this play to be Lear's hypothetical capability, at one stage, "of

---

[7] *Shakespeare 400: Essays by American Scholars on the Anniversary of the Poet's Birth*, ed. by James G. McManaway (New York: Holt, Rinehart and Winston, Inc., 1964), pp. 89–98. See also Professor Heilman's related articles: "Satiety and Conscience: Aspects of Richard III," *Antioch Review*, XXIV (1964), 57–73; "To Know Himself: An Aspect of Tragic Structure," *Review of English Literature*, V (1964), 36–57.

looking fully into the circumambient reality and saying, 'It is I who brought this about,' and 'I brought this about because I am thus and so' " (p. 93). It is Lear's recognition of an error in what he did and in what is within him: the failure of self-illumination to triumph over self-justification. Heilman makes fine employment of this approach, and he cites Yeats to good effect: "Two polar terms of Yeats's come to mind here: 'the quarrel with others' and 'the quarrel with ourselves.' Lear passionately pursues one, hurries over the other" (p. 93). We shall indeed see that this recognition that he, rather than others, is "wrong" is a part of Lear's self-discovery, but I would suggest that it is not the most important part. Nevertheless, even within the brief compass of this article, Heilman's insights are some of the best we have. They benefit especially from dramatic perspective. He cites *Oedipus Rex, Doctor Faustus, The Infernal Machine,* and (as a negative example) *The Death of a Salesman.*

Other writers have more casually referred to self-discovery in *Lear,* demonstrating that it is almost impossible to write about the play without mentioning the subject and also almost impossible to write about the subject without betraying one's individual notion of self-discovery. For most people, apparently, self-discovery means acknowledging that one has erred. This is a reassuring disclosure about the morality of critics, but it has, nonetheless, contributed to the formation of a stereotype.

Theodore Spencer, noting that "*Nosce teipsum* was a piece of advice to which King Lear had never paid any attention," takes the expression to mean the opposite of "lacking in wisdom," that is, doing "nothing good or sensible," leading "a life composed of hasty imperious decisions, based on an unthinking acceptance of his own importance and of what was due him as king and father." [8] Though partly right, this interpretation is a disappointing one considering the subject of Spencer's book: "the nature of man," in which he so influentially probes, in the introductory chapters, into one of the most important Renaissance connotations of the subject. There is very little of this background material

[8] *Shakespeare and the Nature of Man* (New York: Macmillan Company, 1949), p. 140.

in his chapter on *King Lear*. And one regrets that he should interpret Lear's lack of insight as mainly the failure to behave sensibly, or the habit of making hasty decisions. This interpretation of *nosce teipsum* as prudential wisdom can lead critics to the conclusion that Lear makes no self-discovery at all.

This is, in fact, the stimulating but of course impossible argument of an article by Warren Taylor. This article is in large part a rhapsodic and gratuitous attack on historical criticism, but there is a seemingly good point in the following excerpt:

> Unlike his handling of Antony and Othello, whom he permits to voice their own errors in judgment, Shakespeare never permits a full sense of his failures in both his family and his kingdom to cross Lear's consciousness. Shakespeare has him state his regret for his stupid misjudgment of Cordelia and the consequent injustice to her. After Lear recovers from his madness, however, Shakespeare does not grant him any awareness of the condition of his kingdom following his division of it, and more than that, any concern for it, whether tranquil or turbulent. . . . He still has a sense that dutiful daughters should pamper old fathers; this time, the right one will. That is just about as far as Shakespeare goes within Lear's restored consciousness.[9]

Here, certainly, is the disastrous result of interpreting self-insight to mean only "I have made a mistake." All that Taylor says is true enough, except for the conclusion, and this is not based upon full evidence. Certainly Lear overlooks, as Shakespeare himself probably did, many of the practical errors he made. These are about as important to the "moral" of the play as *Gorboduc* (since Taylor cites the dividing of the kingdom) is as a source. Lear is still, in worldly matters, pathetically unwise or unchanged at the end of the play. He would still be unable to fend for himself. As an old man, he may want still to be cherished—unrealistically. He has not learned the wisdom of a Polonius. But he has learned that which, especially for a dying man, is all-important.

A few critics have gone beyond the right-wrong antithesis to

---

[9] "Lear and the Lost Self," *College English*, XXV (1964), 511–512.

some of the less tangible things about himself which Lear has
learned. Manfred Weidhorn, in an article discussing Lear's learning generally, finds that the self-knowledge part of his learning is
summed up in Lear's statement "I am old and foolish." [10] Jo-
sephine Waters Bennett, although beginning with the interpretation that Lear does not know "his own best interests," proceeds to
a profounder concept of Lear's advance in self-insight. Recognizing that "the core of the play is not what happens *to* Lear but
what happens *within* Lear," she remarks that "the storm within
Lear's mind goes beyond good and evil, beyond the narrow world
of preceptoral morality, to the imponderable realities of cause and
effect, of man's ignorance, his weakness, his blindness, and his
blundering and suffering through life to his release from 'the rack
of this tough world.'" This, as we shall see, is largely self-
knowledge in the Renaissance sense. Also illuminating is Mrs.
Bennett's statement that the real story of *King Lear* "is the struggle of a man to retain the self, the stature and the dignities he has
achieved—'Ay, every inch a king'—against the grasping hands of
the next generation and the very forces of nature." [11]

One of the critics most poetically adequate to the explication of
King Lear—whatever we may think of the strict accuracy of his
critical method—is G. Wilson Knight. "But slenderly known himself" means to Knight, it would at first seem, being "wrong-
headed." But Knight's real perception comes in his description of
what Lear succeeds in discovering about himself. "In madness,"
Knight writes, "thoughts deep-buried come to the surface":

*His thoughts fix on the sex-inhibitions of civilized man, delving
into the truth of man's civilized ascent. He finds sex to be a pivot
force in human affairs, sugared though it be by convention. All
human civilization and justice are a mockery. He is all the time
working deep into that which is real, in him or others, facing truth,
though it be hideous. He has been forced from a deceiving con-*

[10] "Lear's Schoolmasters," *Shakespeare Quarterly*, XIII (1962), 313.

[11] "The Storm Within: The Madness of Lear," *Shakespeare Quarterly*, XIII
(1962), 151–154.

sciousness built of self-deception, sentiment, the tinsel of kingship and authority, to the knowledge of his own and others' nature.[12]

To accept Knight's picture as *self*-discovery by Lear, one must recognize a psychological axiom not mentioned by Knight: What one learns about the rottenness of the macrocosm is in part at least simply an extension of what one learns about the microcosm. Renaissance thought would accommodate, though not with the fullest of modern interpretations, this view. What Knight says about sex in the play is not quite so "unhistorical" as it might at first seem to be.

Finally, there are the Christian critics who see Lear's self-discovery as coming nothing short of redemption or salvation. According to Roy W. Battenhouse, one of the most sober and learned of the theological critics, "the achievement of self-understanding in any final sense waits upon Christian apocalypse." [13] There is, of course, the difficulty that *King Lear* is set in pagan times and most of the references are to the gods rather than to God. Battenhouse believes, however, that there are Christian elements in the play and that a pagan subject does not rule out a Christian overview:

A Christian view of pagan history can discern in the panorama of that history a place for nihilistic, stoic, and other attitudes. These can be seen by a Christian dramatist as variant responses to life's trials through which pagans (and we too in our potentially pagan moments) typically stumble into disaster but then, more hopefully, can grope upward toward self-understanding.

(p. 175)

One does not have to have a written scripture or an institutional church to make men seek the knowledge necessary for salvation.

[12] "The *Lear* Universe," in *The Wheel of Fire: Interpretations of Shakespearean Tragedy, With Three New Essays* (Cleveland and New York: World Publishing Company, 1957), p. 200. Originally published in 1930.
[13] "Shakespeare's Moral Vision," *Stratford Papers on Shakespeare, 1964* (Toronto: Published for McMaster University by W. J. Gage Limited, 1965), p. 175.

The earth itself, as Cordelia says, has "unpublish'd virtues," and nature can, through adversity, lead Christians to the requisite knowledge.

This kind of criticism has been much maligned of late, particularly in its tendency to find allegory. Cordelia, for instance, is often seen as a Christ figure. According to S. L. Bethell, one of the most influential proponents of the allegorical method,

Cordelia, whom Shakespeare has made "Christian"—or indeed Christ-like—holds a position of central importance in the play, since she symbolizes the goal of Lear's purgatorial struggle. She is the good that he rejected in blind pride, and to which, in the new wisdom gained of suffering and sorrow, he was enabled to return, recognizing for the first time her true nature as "a soul in bliss." [14]

In similar vein, Paul N. Siegel sees Cordelia as a Christ figure symbolic of Lear's redemption and affirms that "Lear's final conviction that Cordelia is alive might be regarded as the mysterious insight believed to be granted a man on the point of death, the last blessing conferred upon him as he is kneeling by the corpse of his daughter." [15]

In a book seeking to ascertain the theological soundness of the religiously oriented critics, Roland Mushat Frye briefly disposes of the contention that there is much self-knowledge, in the Christian sense, in Shakespeare, except perhaps for that which Gertrude partially attains under the excoriating sermon of Hamlet.[16] Although Frye's study does not take adequately into account what Bryant calls the Elizabethan habit of "analogical thinking" (p. 114), it

[14] *Shakespeare and the Popular Dramatic Tradition* (London: Staples Press, 1948), pp. 60–61.

[15] *Shakespearean Tragedy and the Elizabethan Compromise* (New York: New York University Press, 1957), p. 185. For other religious interpretations see J. A. Bryant, Jr. *Hippolyta's View: Some Christian Aspects of Shakespeare's Plays* (Lexington: University of Kentucky Press, 1961) though this is not specifically on *King Lear;* Oscar James Campbell, "The Salvation of Lear," *ELH,* XV (1948), 93–109; John Danby, "'King Lear' and Christian Patience," *Cambridge Journal,* I (1948), 305–320; Irving Ribner, *Patterns in Shakespearian Tragedy* (New York: Barnes & Noble, Inc., 1960), pp. 116–136.

[16] *Shakespeare and Christian Doctrine* (Princeton: Princeton University Press, 1965), pp. 247–249.

serves as a useful check upon the sometimes inspired and excited interpretations of the religious critics. Theologically, however, it is limited to the writings of Luther, Calvin, and Hooker; and for the subject of self-knowledge, it goes very slightly into these three writers. Frye has apparently overlooked entirely the considerable body of writings dealing more specifically and at greater length than Luther or Hooker with the subject of self-knowledge in a Christian context. These are discussed in chapter ii, but I cannot promise any conclusive word on the vexing and sometimes bitterly controversial subject of the Christian interpretation of Shakespearean tragedy. I am compelled to deal with it because it is a strong possibility in a full understanding of Lear's self-discovery and because Renaissance treatises on *nosce teipsum* seldom fail to stress it.

II
Some Renaissance Contexts

The comments of the critics cited in chapter i make it clear that self-knowledge is a part of Lear's quest which can hardly be ignored in any approach to the play. They make it even clearer that, except for the theologically oriented critics, there is little agreement as to what self-knowledge meant to Shakespeare beyond the ability to see that one has made a mistake in judgment or that one has done wrong. It would be helpful not only to this immediate subject but to the total interpretation of Shakespeare's greatest play if we had some certain guide to Shakespeare's meaning apart from the play. It is, however, the essential and obdurate nature of Shakespeare's artistry that no external clue, not even a "source," is an infallible guide to interpretation. But before I proffer my own approach to the subject—in which I shall attempt a greater range of perspective than casual commentary has previously permitted critics—I wish to survey a body of Renaissance writings that are more relevant to the subject than any others I know. Moreover, they have been almost totally overlooked.[1]

I am aware that the history of ideas, with the rare exceptions of scholars like Theodore Spencer, E. M. W. Tillyard, and Willard Farnham, has not been applied to Shakespearean interpretation with universal approbation. "Historical" scholars, who seek to find the meaning of Shakespeare through a study of Renaissance thought, have found their principal reward, in view of the monotonously uniform reaction of reviewers, in the incontestably

---

[1] A few are alluded to by Sidney Warhaft in "Bacon and the Renaissance Ideal of Self-Knowledge," *Personalist*, XLIV (1963), 454–471, but Warhaft does not seem to have had access to the many rare books that deal specifically with *nosce teipsum*. Lily B. Campbell, in *Shakespeare's Tragic Heroes: Slaves of Passion* (New York: Barnes & Noble, Inc., 1952), pp. 103-106, takes the subject to mean mainly physiognomy, cites Aristotle and Thomas Betterton, but fails to mention any Renaissance writers in this section. She is, however, perhaps the first modern scholar to perceive that *nosce teipsum* was "the absorbing problem of the Renaissance" (p. 103).

superior quantity of labor they have put into their work as compared with the purely literary critics. The wiser of them acknowledge that there is some truth in the reviewers' misapplication of
Ben Jonson's words, "not of an age but for all time," and turn, not
always so regretfully as one would hope, to view Shakespeare in
terms not of "all time" but of their own age—a procedure that, if
it does not produce Thomas Rymers, is a sensible one. What,
therefore, I have to say about the age's view, or views, of self-
knowledge is presented with diffidence and only as a suggestive
background. My aim is to present not one, but several perspectives
on the subject. My only certain conviction is that Shakespeare
himself had a similar flexibility of approach.

II

In order to supply a historical approach, I began searching in
books written in the late sixteenth and early seventeenth centuries
for casual references to self-knowledge. I knew, of course, from the
outset that there was one philosophical poem dealing specifically
and at some length with the subject: Sir John Davies' *Nosce
Teipsum* (1599). I was surprised to find that there were at least
two other volumes whose titles indicated that their whole subject
too was self-knowledge: Philippe de Mornay's *The True Knowledge of a Mans Owne Selfe*, translated by Anthony Munday in
1602, and John Frith's *A Mirrour or Glasse to Know Thyselfe* (ca.
1533). I knew also that Augustine had written on the question of
whether a man could learn to know himself. And of course
Montaigne, though he had written no essays on the subject, was
one of the first to *illustrate* self-examination in his own writings. I
was aware that his introspective approach, well known by Shakespeare, would have served as at least a stimulus.

But these proved to be only beginnings. Instead of scattered
references—and I found many of these in the sermons of the time,
including the official homilies—I discovered at least ten other
books that dealt substantially, often at the beginning, with the
subject. Most of these were written either before *King Lear* or at

approximately the same time. *Nosce teipsum* was a popular subject for books when Shakespeare was conceiving his play. He would not, I think, have pointed explicitly to the hazard of imperfectly knowing oneself nor would he have had his hero ask in one of his most emphatic lines "Who is it that can tell me who I am?" without at least some awareness that he was alluding to a subject treated in more than a dozen books of the time. This does not mean, of course, that he was merely repeating the ideas of these books. It is more likely that he would have used some of them, but still more likely that he would have had his own views to express on a subject of great current interest.

These treatises dealing with *nosce teipsum* have, furthermore, one important feature in common: they include a section, sometimes called an exhortation, stressing the urgent importance of their subject. A part of their motive for this may have been merely self-advertisement. *Nosce teipsum* was a popular subject, and it was a good sales point to emphasize it. Indeed, it is not unlikely that one or two of the authors said their books dealt importantly with self-knowledge when in fact they were more concerned with other things. But the exhortations are, nonetheless, illuminating. For the most part they seem urgent and admonitory, befitting guides to what the writers considered the most important of topics.

Pierre Charron typically begins his work *Of Wisdome* (translated *ca.* 1612) with what he calls "An Exhortation to the studie and knowledge of our selves":

The most excellent and divine counsell, the best and most profitable advertisment of all others, but the least practised, is to study and learne how to know our selves; This is the foundation of Wisdome and the high way to whatsoever is good; and there is no folly comparable to this, To be painfull and diligent to know all things els, whatsoever rather than our selves. For the true science and studie of man, is man himselfe.

(p. 1)

This "exhortation" is also typical in what seems to us its vacuity. But those who know Renaissance books of moral philosophy are aware that there can be substance in their very earnestness. And when Charron proceeds with his exhortation, we find pointed details that are not irrelevant to the meaning of *King Lear*: "God, Nature, the wise, the world, preach man and exhort him both by word and deed to the studie and knowledge of himselfe. . . . Nature hath enjoyned this worke unto all" (pp. 1–2). With the doubtful exception of God, Charron has in fact pointed to those agents in *King Lear* which "preach man and exhort him" to self-discovery. Charron also makes it clear that study of oneself comprises study of man. This he had stressed earlier: "The first book teacheth the knowledge of our selves and our *humane condition,* which is the foundation of Wisdome, by five great and principall considerations of man, and containeth 62. Chapters" (sig. A8ʳ). Another exhortation, that by Pierre Boaistuau in *Theatrum Mundi* (1581), points out that man has been able to understand and put to use wild beasts and herbs and plants, yet "notwithstanding he is of himself so masked and disguised that he knoweth not himselfe" (The Epistle Dedicatorie). It is unlikely that Boaistuau had a very sophisticated notion of "masked and disguised"; certainly it would not include the fullness of meaning demanded by modern psychology and literary criticism and so brilliantly dramatized in *King Lear*. Nevertheless, Boaistuau is, I think, an overlooked and not unimportant source for ideas and perhaps passages in *King Lear*. He is an intelligent and subtle writer, not unworthy of comparison in parts with Montaigne, with whom he is contemporary.

Of the exhortations the favorite feature, because it is the most alarming, is the admonition. If audiences had these admonitions in mind when they witnessed *King Lear*, they would have felt the full ominousness of Regan's "yet he hath ever but slenderly known himself." Here is a typical admonition, taken from Lodowick Bryskett's *A Discourse of Civill Life; Containing the Ethike Part of Morall Philosophie* (1606):

And as this [self-]knowledge is of all other things most properly appertaining to humaine wisedome; so is the neglecting thereof the greatest and most harmfull folly of all others: for from the *said knowledge . . . spring all virtues and goodnes; even as from the ignorance thereof flow all vices and evils that are among men.*

(p. 163)

Similarly Bishop Abernethy, discussing "that vocation to employ our thoughts on our selves," warns that failure to so employ ourselves leads to "a habite of false principles, and false opinions" which is damnable: "This is an ignorance of our selves, both *miserable and abominable. It is a most fearefull plague. The Lord smiteth many with madnesse, and blindnesse, and with astonying of heart.*" [2] Here it is interesting, though the work could not have influenced *King Lear*, that two of the penalties of self-ignorance are cited as madness and blindness. At any rate, if Bryskett and Abernethy and their fellow writers were correct, the tragedy that befalls Lear is not excessive for a man who lacked self-knowledge.

III

Despite the fact that lack of self-knowledge is a damnable sin, most writers of the treatises dealing with *nosce teipsum* agree that it is a very difficult one to avoid. The principal reason for this is the decline of man's reason since the Fall. Though, as Abernethy points out (p. 19), the mind has lost some of its power to study nature, much of this kind of power can be recovered. "But the immanent beames reflected on our selves, whereby we should behold, contemplate and study our selves (which is both great Philosophy, and a beginning of Theologie) are farre more darkened." The audience would have heard this message repeatedly in sermons.[3] And

---

[2] John Abernethy, *A Christian and Heavenly Treatise, Containing Physicke for the Soule* (3d ed., 1622), pp. 20–21. This work, first published in 1615, makes an extensive Christian interpretation of self-knowledge. The "habite of false principles, and false opinions" is merely one of the kinds of self-ignorance the Bishop discusses.

[3] John Hooper, declaring that "it is very difficile and hard for man to know himself," maintains that "the only way thereunto is to examine and open himself before God by the light of the scripture." *A Declaration of Christe in His Office* (1555), in *Early Writings of John Hooper, D. D.*, ed. by Rev. Samuel Carr (Cambridge: The University Press, 1843), p. 88.

there is of course a reference to the Fall in *King Lear*. A Gentleman tells the King:

> Thou hast one daughter
> Who redeems Nature from the general curse
> Which twain have brought her to.

(IV.vi.209–211)

For the allegorical critics this could easily suggest, as Lear is at this
point achieving self-knowledge, that Cordelia (a Christ figure) is
restoring, or is a symbol of the restoration of, Lear's insight. But
the allegorical critics seem mostly not to have read the sermons
and treatises that deal with man's loss of self-knowledge since the
Fall, and I do not wish to carry alone the full responsibility for this
interpretation, especially since Shakespeare is parsimonious of further clues.

The difficulty of achieving self-knowledge is made more relevant
to *King Lear* by John Davies of Hereford in *Microcosmos* (1603),
a work whose title indicates that it is largely concerned with man's
study of himself. Davies writes:

> If not impossible, yet hard it is,
> For the most learn'd and lowly wel to know
> Themselves in ev'ry part, and not to misse;
> Then sith the Prowd doe never looke so low
> That skil nere comes but with their overthrow:
> For they by nature are most prone to pride
> That know all but themselves; and yet doe show
> They know themselves too wel, for, nought beside
> They love; which love, that knowledge doth misguide.[4]

Pride and self-love, rather than the Fall (though these are closely
connected), thus are seen as making it especially difficult for man
to know himself. And flatterers can aggravate man's (and especially a king's) proneness to blinding pride. As a king, Lear had
been flattered since his youth:

---

[4] In *The Complete Works of John Davies of Hereford*, ed. by A. B. Grosart
(Edinburgh: T. and A. Constable, 1878), I, 77.

They flatter'd me like a dog, and told me I had the white hairs in
my beard ere the black ones were there. To say "ay" and "no" to
everything that I said! . . . they told me I was everything. . . .

(IV.vi.97–106)

Abernethy remarked that if self-blindness is accompanied by "daily
flattery, it is the more desperate" (p. 26). And Erasmus, though
his book is not specifically on self-knowledge, but on the general
education needed for a prince, is one of the best guides that Lear
might have had. Erasmus is especially fervent on the subject of
flatterers, for these lead to a specious enlargement of one's ego as
king. What one gains by flattery as a king is no true guide to an
estimate of oneself:

Judge yourself, not on your physical appearance or by your good
fortune, but on the qualities of your spirit. Measure yourself, not
by the commendations of others, but by the standard of your own
deeds. Since you are a prince, do not admit of any commendations
which are not worthy a prince. . . . If anyone extols your lofty
station, this should be your thought: "He would praise me rightly
if there were something to be taken from my high place." [5]

One of the things Lear must learn is the self-knowledge based
upon his being a man rather than upon being a king.

IV

If flattery and pride make self-knowledge especially difficult, it is
to be expected—and the treatises grimly confirm this fact—that
the surest guide to self-knowledge is affliction. John Davies of
Hereford, we recall, had said:

Then sith the Prowd doe never looke so low
That skil nere comes but with their overthrow.

---

[5] Desiderius Erasmus, Education of a Christian Prince, trans. by Lester K.
Born (New York: Columbia University Press, 1936), p. 188. Erasmus also
notes (p. 196), "There are two periods of life which are especially susceptible
to flattery: extreme youth because of its inexperience, and old age because of its
weakness."

Affliction, he adds (I, 36), makes "us know our selves at the first sight / And bring'st us to our selves, our selves to see." In *Nosce Teipsum* Sir John Davies writes to similar purpose:

> If aught can teach us aught, afflictions looks,
> Making us look into ourselves so near,
> Teach us to know ourselves beyond all books,
> Or all the learned Schools that ever were.[6]

What affliction teaches that man must learn for self-knowledge is conveniently summed up by Myles Coverdale after stating "that it is a profitable and a good thing for a man to know himself well":

Felicity and prosperity blindeth a man; but when he is under the cross he beginneth to mark the frailness of his body, the uncertainty of his life, the feebleness of his understanding, the infirmity and weakness of man's strength and power.[7]

These happen to be some of the most important things Lear must learn; and it is of some significance that they are prescribed by a divine. But one need not have been a divine to recognize, in general terms, that affliction leads to self-knowledge. One of the most grandly secular of all Elizabethans, Sir Walter Ralegh, had the opportunity through his study of history and through his personal ordeal to learn what self-knowledge entailed in terms of suffering. In a noble passage from his *History of the World*, he affirms that it is nothing short of death itself which can teach true self-knowledge:

It was Death, which opening the conscience of Charles the Fifth, made him enjoin his son Philip to restore Navarre; and king Francis the First of France, to command that justice should be

---

[6] In *Silver Poets of the Sixteenth Century*, ed. by Gerald Bullett (London: J. M. Dent & Sons, Ltd., 1955), p. 349.

[7] *A Spiritual and Most Precious Perle* (1550), in *Writings and Translations of Myles Coverdale*, ed. by Rev. George Pearson (Cambridge: The University Press, 1844), p. 119. See also Hugh Latimer, *A Sermon Preached by Master Hugh Latimer, the Fourth Sunday after the Epiphany and the Last Day of January, Anno 1552*, in *Sermons and Remains of Hugh Latimer*, ed. by Rev. George E. Corrie (Cambridge: The University Press, 1845), p. 185.

done upon the murderers of the protestants in Merindol and Cabrieres, which till then he neglected. *It is therefore Death alone that can suddenly make man to know himself. He tells the proud and insolent, that they are but abjects, and humbles them at the instant, makes them cry, complain, and repent, yea, even to hate their forepast happiness. He takes the account of the rich, and proves him a beggar, a naked beggar, which hath interest in nothing but in the gravel that fills his mouth. He holds a glass before the eyes of the most beautiful, and makes them see therein their deformity and rottenness, and they acknowledge it.*[8]

Much of what Ralegh says that the autocratic and proud learn is true of Lear, especially his equating himself with the "naked beggar"; but it is one of the big and unanswerable questions of *King Lear* criticism whether *at the moment of his dying* Lear has accurate perceptions.

V

It is, however, time to turn to a more detailed consideration of what the Renaissance treatises meant by self-knowledge. We recall that many of the modern commentators on self-knowledge in *King Lear* interpret it to mean recognition of an error in judgment. This interpretation is indeed found in the Renaissance treatises. Charron, in fact, has a passage on the subject which bears so closely upon Lear's defect in judgment that it merits extensive quotation. There is a further reason for seeing at length what Charron has to say. Though S. Lennard's English translation was not entered before 1606 and not published much before 1612, it may have been available to Shakespeare in manuscript. Furthermore, the French original was published in 1601, and there is almost as much likelihood of Shakespeare's having read this as the French original of Charron's more influential friend Montaigne. Charron's is one of

[8] *The History of the World*, Book V, chap. vi, in *The Works of Sir Walter Ralegh, Kt.* (New York: Burt Franklin [1964]; originally published 1829), VII, 900.

the most informative treatises on self-knowledge. Of the man defective in judgment, he writes:

He that shall call to minde how often he hath miscarried in his judgement . . . shall learn thereby to trust it no more. He that shall note how often he hath held an opinion, and in such sort understood a thing even to the engaging of his owne credit, and the satisfying of himselfe and any other therein, and that afterwards time hath made him see the truth even the contrarie to that he formerly held, may learne to distrust his owne judgement, and to shake off that importunate arrogancie and querulous presumption. . . . He that shall well note and consider all those evils that he hath run into, that hath threatened him; the light occasions that have altered his course and turned him from one estate to another; how often repentances and mislikes have come into his heart; will prepare himselfe against future changes, learne to knowe his owne condition.[9]

(*Of Wisdome, p. 3*)

In Lear we find "importunate arrogancie and querulous presumption." We find also "the light occasions that have altered his course and turned him from one estate to another."

Undoubtedly Lear's tragedy, insofar as it proceeds from self-ignorance, is partly the result of such defect of judgment. But what must be noted further is that the defective judgment is seldom, in the Renaissance, stressed as the basic fault. It is merely the consequence of inordinate passions (and, according to some writers, the fall of man). Charron explains it thus:

. . . the will is made to follow the understanding as a guide and lampe unto it; but being so corrupted and seized on by the force of the passions (or rather by the fall of our first father Adam) doth likewise perhaps corrupt the understanding, and so from hence come the greatest part of our erroneous judgements.

(p. 66)

Similarly Philippe de Mornay in his *The True Knowledge of a Mans Owne Selfe*: "The knowledge of a mans owne selfe,

---

[9] See also Abernethy, p. 25.

availeth . . . to moderate the vehemencie of inordinate affec-
tions, which hinder and impeach the health of judgement." There
is certainly much justification for Lily B. Campbell's study of *King
Lear* as a tragedy of wrath in old age.

What is important to recognize here is that, from the point of
view of self-knowledge, it is the passions and not the judgment
which are the real villains. Thus, though by "he hath ever but
slenderly known himself" is meant partly Goneril's term for it,
"poor judgement" in casting off Cordelia, the expression is clari-
fied when Goneril proceeds to link it with "the unruly wayward-
ness that infirm and choleric years bring with them." Old age,
among other things, has aggravated his choler, and this has led, as
the dramatic action makes clear, to faulty judgment. Lear's error in
self-knowledge here was in not understanding his passions; these
constitute a substantial part of *nosce teipsum* treatises. This is true
of Thomas Rogers' *A Philosophicall Discourse Entituled, The
Anatomie of the Minde* (1576), which takes up anger, wrath, and
lust, among other passions; and it is strikingly true of Thomas
Wright's *The Passions of the Minde* (1604), which has a chapter
(Book III, chap. 1) entitled "Means for every man to know his
own passions." According to Wright, "Before all other things, it is
most necessary for him that will moderate or mortifie his Passions,
to know his owne Inclination, and to what Passions his Soule most
bendeth" (p. 78). "Another remedy to know thy selfe," according
to Wright (p. 79), "more palpable to be perceived," is to mark
passions in other men. But the observation by Wright most
applicable to *King Lear* is the following:

*It chanceth sometimes, by Gods permission, that our enemies
(who prie into our actions and examine more narrowly our inten-
tions then wee our selves) discover unto us better our Passions,
and reveale our imperfections, then ever we our selves.*

(p. 80)

To a considerable extent Lear's self-education is the result of a
canny, but limited, study—at first better than he himself can
make—of his vulnerable passions by his enemies (and also his
friends).

VI

More important for an understanding of self-knowledge in *King Lear* than the passionately misdirected judgment is the fact that the books on *nosce teipsum* are deeply interested in the human body. This is not just the body of the one who would learn to know himself, but of man's (and woman's) body in general. Boaistuau would make knowledge of the body central to *nosce teipsum:*

Man to my judgement, hath inough wherein to exercise himselfe, if he wil with a vigilant eye behold the stratagem of mans body as also an infinit number of calamities & miseries, wherewith he is wrapped even from his birth unto his grave.

(*The Epistle Dedicatorie*)

Many other writers in this genre "behold the stratagem of mans body." A few of them seem to be writing mainly texts on physiology. Thomas Walkington manages, in *The Optick Glasse of Humors* (1607), to make such a physiology qualify as a *nosce teipsum* book, since, as he argues, the body is "the edifice or handmaid of the soule" and leads to knowledge of the soul (sig. B2^v). De Mornay's *The True Knowledge of a Mans Owne Selfe* is also largely concerned with the body. His English translator, Anthony Munday, explains that the glass that De Mornay has provided for looking into oneself

discovers the inward parts of the bodie, from the very houre of conception, to the latest minute of life, with the manner of nourishing, increasing and growing to perfection, and how the body naturally liveth by his power & organes, with every sence, nerve and faculty thereto belonging.

(sig. A12^r)

An interesting feature of this book is that, like Davies' *Nosce Teipsum* and like La Primaudaye's *The French Academie* (which

Louis Bredvold has shown to be an important source for Davies [10]),
it leads to the conclusion, as Munday says, that "the soule
hath her being in the body, approving the dignitie and immor-
talitie thereof." It is doubtless only accidental that at least three of
the books concerned with *nosce teipsum* have as their procedure a
study of the body leading to an affirmation of its immortality. One
longs to find this significant also for *King Lear*, but mortality is
only too grimly emphatic a part of what we, and Lear, feel at the
end of the play ("Thou'lt come no more, / Never, never, never,
never, never!"). What is more certain is that knowledge of the
body was considered very important in the process of self-discovery. One divine even makes ignorance in this respect theologically
dangerous. According to Abernethy (p. 20), "this sort of ignorance of our selves is miserable, yet it is not sinne, but a part of our
misery, and punishment of sinne."

What our bodies could teach us about ourselves consisted principally of two things: the body's infirmity and man's basic needs.
Thomas Rogers writes:

. . . *he who throughly would know him selfe, must aswell knowe
his boddie, as his minde. The boddie to put him in minde, of his
slaverie: the minde of his felicitie. . . . Then it is meete that we
knowe our boddies what they are, what their goods, and what their
friends. . . .*

(*To the Reader*)

Much of this is of course medieval *de contemptu mundi*, but it
has been incorporated into a Renaissance context. Man must
know his body's limitations as means for survival on this earth.
This is made clearer by Charron:

. . . *he that knowes not his owne infirmities, takes no care to
amend them; he that is ignorant of his owne wants, takes no care
to amend them; he that feeles not his owne evils and miseries, ad-
viseth not with himselfe of helps, nor seeks for remedie. . . .*

[10] See Louis I. Bredvold, "The Sources Used by Davies in *Nosce Teipsum*,"
PMLA, XXXVIII (1923), 745–769.

Thou must of necessitie know thy selfe, before thou amend thy selfe. . . .

(p. 4)

Learning man's "infirmities and wants," as Abernethy calls them (p. 25), is an important and practical part of self-knowledge for the here and now. Lear, as we shall see at some length in the last chapter, must learn "the art of our necessities."

Nevertheless, the treatises take predominantly a medieval view (sometimes modified by Calvinism) of the frailty, wretchedness, and corruption of the flesh. Sir John Davies, immediately after stating, "Only myself I study, learn, and know," turns to the body's frailty:

> I know my body's of so frail a kind
> As force without, fevers within, can kill.

(p. 350)

Boaistuau, to show the vulnerability of man's body, paraphrases Pliny's *Natural History*. As this passage bears so closely upon Lear's "unaccommodated man" speech, it is worth quoting at moderate length:

> Let us consider a little (sayth hee) how it behooveth man to cover his bodye, at the dispensation of other beastes. . . . And yet the better to shew in what contempt nature hath man, she hath brought him forth alone, naked upon the earth disdainfully, as a fruit out of time, and at the first houre of his birth hath assigned him teres for his heritance, which are as forerunners and messengers for his calamities to come. Behold heere the chief and head of the works of nature, & for whom all other things are created, which is so weake of himself, that if he be left without the helpe and succour of others, hee should be devoured of other beasts.

(p. 11)

There follows a comparison of man and beasts which is of relevance to the celebrated "beast theme" in *King Lear*, but which is not so relevant to our study of man's frail and corrupt body. Whether Shakespeare used this paraphrase rather than Pliny (whom he used elsewhere [11]) is likewise not vital to our inquiry, though an interesting question. Pliny has, in Philemon Holland's translation (1601), "cry and wraule" (p. 152), which is closer to Shakespeare than Boaistuau's "teres for his heritance." On the other hand, where Holland's Pliny has *"living creatures* live orderly and well," Boaistuau has "other *beasts,"* and repeatedly uses *beasts.* For the helpless nakedness of man as compared to animals, the matter of influence is further complicated by the demonstrable fact that Shakespeare knew Montaigne, and George Coffin Taylor has documented the indebtedness in *Shakspere's Debt to Montaigne* (1925). Montaigne, however, is partially in the tradition of the *nosce teipsum* writers; and all I wish to suggest here is that it was a customary function of these writers to instruct man in humility by calling his attention to his frail body and its basic needs.

The religious writers would add to this a stronger emphasis on the corruption of the flesh. Thomas Becon, immediately after stating that the "first point of wisdom, by the common consent of all learned men, is the knowledge of ourselves," makes it clear that this self-knowledge means understanding the vileness of the flesh; we must "know that so many of us as be born of the seed of Adam be born very flesh of flesh, impure, unhallowed, abominable before God." [12]

VII

Understanding of the body was, however, in the school of *nosce teipsum* but a step, albeit an essential one, in the process of learning humility. And we can best approach this aspect of our subject

[11] See Kenneth Muir, *Shakespeare's Sources: I. Comedies and Tragedies* (London: Methuen & Co., Ltd., 1957), p. 127.
[12] *The Newes oute of Heaven Both Pleasaunt and Joyfull, The First Part of the Bokes which Thomas Becon Made and Published in the Name of Theodor Basille* (1560), in *The Early Works of Thomas Becon,* ed. by Rev. John Ayre (Cambridge: The University Press, 1843), p. 42.

by looking at a play written shortly before *King Lear*. This play, *Measure for Measure*, comes perhaps closest to *King Lear* in its concern with self-knowledge. In it, a proud and severely virtuous man (Angelo), a weak sensualist (Claudio), and a severely virtuous woman (Isabella) all are forced to modify their attitudes toward themselves. Both Angelo and Isabella, particularly the former, learn that their exalted images of themselves must be revised downward. Isabella learns that she must be a woman and a sister, as well as a saint; and Angelo learns that he must be a man as well as a model of abstinence. Angelo's self-discovery, though coming much more swiftly and less agonizingly than Lear's, is one of the reasons for the greatness of an otherwise imperfect play.[13] From his successful insight into this proud autocrat of morality and severe justicer, Shakespeare may have gotten part of his inspiration for the fuller and much grander spectacle of the autocratic and unbending Lear learning that he is, before all else, a man.

It is a speech of Isabella's which bears most closely upon the lesson that Angelo (and she also, in part) must learn:

> . . . but man, proud man,
> Dress'd in a little brief authority,
> Most ignorant of what he's most assur'd,
> His glassy essence, like an angry ape,
> Plays such fantastic tricks before high heaven
> As makes the angels weep; who, with our spleens,
> Would all themselves laugh mortal.

(II.ii.117–123)

The message here is an elaboration of an idea found in Hooker, among many others. Hooker refers to our tendency "to fawn upon ourselves, and to be ignorant as much as may be of our own deformities, without the feeling sense whereof we are most wretched." [14] (It may be noted here that "the *feeling* sense" of

---

[13] For an examination of the play in terms of Angelo's self-discovery, see W. H. Durham, " 'What Art Thou, Angelo?' " *Studies in the Comic*, University of California Publications in English, VIII (2): 155–174.

[14] Richard Hooker, *Of the Laws of Ecclesiastical Polity* (London: J. M. Dent & Sons Ltd., 1963), I, 210–211. An important case for Hooker's more pervasive

our own deformities is a part of the learning process in *King Lear.*) Isabella's words, driven home by his own sudden insight into his true nature, lead Angelo to ask the question never asked before, I think—certainly not asked with such dramatic intensity —in Shakespeare:

> O, fie, fie, fie!
> What dost thou, or what art thou, Angelo?
> Dost thou desire her foully for those things
> That make her good? . . .
> . . . .
> Ever till now,
> When men were fond, I smil'd and wond'red how.
> (II.ii.172–187)

What Angelo discovers about himself is merely one specific aspect of the larger unpleasant truth described by the Renaissance moralists who wrote on self-knowledge. The humbling message is well put by John Davies of Hereford:

> For who so lookes with well-descerning eies.
> (If he be mortal, be he what he wil)
> Into him selfe, he wil himselfe despise;
> For in him selfe he findeth nought but ill,
> Corrupting Soule and Body, Minde, and Will:
> The best shall finde but matter too too bad
> To humble them, and so to keepe them still;
> The worst shal see ynough to make them mad,
> Seeing themselves through Ill, so ill-bestad.
> (I, 77)

"The best shall finde but matter too too bad / To humble them" is applicable to both Angelo and Lear; and we shall later inquire whether that "matter" is not in Lear, as it clearly is in Angelo, at least partially sex.

influence on Shakespeare has been made by Virgil K. Whitaker, *Shakespeare's Use of Learning: An Inquiry into the Growth of his Mind & Art* (San Marino, Calif.: Huntington Library, 1953), pp. 198–209 and *passim.*

The most general insight applicable to Lear is that one is a man, with all that implies of both good and ill. Rogers writes:

> *It was not for naught then that Philip that most famous of the Macedonians so carefully willed his page every morning at his chamber doore to crie, Philip remember thou art a man: and repeteth these wordes with a most lowde voice three times. . . .*
>
> (*To the Reader*)

Charron cites Socrates as best exemplifying the most important kind of humility in self-knowledge:

> *Socrates was accounted the wisest man of the world, not because his knowledge was more compleat, or his sufficiency greater then others; in that he held himselfe within his owne ranke, and knew better how to play the man. . . . Socrates was but purblinde; for being a man as others were, weake and miserable, he knew it, and ingenuously acknowledged his condition, and lived and governed himselfe according unto it.*
>
> (*p. 5*)

"To play the man" means here not manliness, but the condition and rank of man. Acceptance of one's being a man is likewise the ultimate self-recognition in Sir John Davies' *Nosce Teipsum:*

> And, to conclude, I know myself a MAN,
> Which is a proud, and yet a wretched thing.
>
> (*p. 350*)

The bifurcated nature of man, suggested by Davies, has been well treated by Theodore Spencer and Herschel Baker, among others; and I do not need to do more than recommend reemphasis of what these scholars have said so well. But it needs to be stressed also that the writers on self-knowledge—and it is these with whom we are most concerned—almost invariably take one's self-recognition as a man not to be a "proud," but a "wretched thing"—as in "proud man, / Dress'd in a little brief authority, / Most ignorant of what he's most assur'd, / His glassy essence. . . ." And for a study of *King Lear*, this is what most matters. In *Hamlet* there may be the tension between the pessimistic and the optimistic views of man which Spencer so ably analyzes. But it is significant that he drops this theory when he comes to *King Lear*.

Self-discovery, at least as we find it in the Renaissance treatises, simply did not mean learning that man is a splendid creature. A few philosophers do make this interpretation, but it is a faintly minority voice. John Calvin, who has two substantial sections on *nosce teipsum* in his *Institutes of the Christian Religion* and who was one of the most influential shapers of the Renaissance attitude toward the subject, writes of the "correct" interpretation at the beginning of Book II. After endorsing the crucial importance of the precept urging self-knowledge, he proceeds:

> But since this precept is so valuable, we ought more diligently to avoid applying it perversely. This, we observe, has happened to certain philosophers, who, while urging man to know himself, propose the goal of recognizing his own worth and excellence. And they would have him contemplate in himself nothing but what swells him with empty assurance and puffs him up with pride.
>
> But knowledge of ourselves lies first in considering what we were given at creation. . . . Secondly to call to mind our miserable condition after Adam's fall; the awareness of which, when all our boasting and self-assurance are laid low, should truly humble us and overwhelm us with shame.[15]

In his earlier section on self-knowledge, Calvin had written: "For we always seem to ourselves righteous and upright and wise and holy—the pride is innate in all of us—unless by clear proofs we stand convinced of our own unrighteousness, foulness, folly, and impurity" (I, 37).

Most of the writers whom I have read—and I have tried to read most of those who deal extensively with self-knowledge—would agree with Calvin. His message is, to cite only one example, very pronounced in John Frith's *A Mirrour or Glasse to Know Thyselfe*. Like his fellow writers, Frith finds that the Scriptures support self-knowledge as "the chefest poynt of wysdome and direccyon of a mannes lyfe." And the Scriptures teach, Frith says,

[15] Ed. by John T. McNeill, trans. by Ford Lewis Battles (Philadelphia: Westminster Press, 1960), I, 241–242.

that there is no hope for him as a man "yf I perceyve not the im-
perfection of my nature which is subjecte unto corrupcyon & voyde
of all stablenes: If I perceyve not the unstablenes of my flesh
beeing prone to all synne, & rebellyous to ryghteousnes, and that
there dwelleth no goodnes in me" (sig. A3ᵛ).

I need not here go into the numerous religious treatises that
assert the only means to self-knowledge is to study one's own
sins.[16] These are significant, surely, but are not so important as
those that interpret self-knowledge to consist of recognition of
man's miserable condition. Roland Mushat Frye can find little of
the conventional kind of religious self-knowledge in Shakespeare,
including *King Lear.* But perhaps he defines Christian self-
knowledge too narrowly: "the knowledge of one's own sin, and the
need for God's grace" (p. 247). Lear may not seem to be closely
examining his own personal sins, but he *is* examining the sinful-
ness of man and woman. And we shall later see that he does so
through the topics customary to the Renaissance treatises—the
frailty and corruption of the body.

VIII

Whether or not the treatises go still further and support the
modern theological critics in finding salvation in *King Lear* as the
final stage of self-knowledge is a thornier question. Almost all that
can be said in the affirmative is that salvation is quite commonly
looked upon as the end of self-knowledge. Thus, near the beginning of *The French Academie* (1594), which provides one of the
most conventional treatments of self-knowledge, La Primaudaye
writes: "Truelie yee have reasons (companions) to begin our
happie assemblie with that knowledge, which we ought to have
of our selves, as being the storehouse of all wisedome, and beginning of salvation" (pp. 10–11). For, La Primaudaye adds, self-

---

[16] See, for three examples, William Perkins, *The Estate of a Christian in this
Life,* in *Works* (Cambridge, 1605), pp. 433–434; Thomas Becon, *The Path-
waie unto Prayer,* ed. cit., p. 145; John Norden, *A Progresse of Pietie* (1596),
(Cambridge: The University Press, 1847), pp. 47–48.

knowledge is "a guide to leade him [man] to the true knowledge of God." But how does this specifically lead to salvation? Calvin had written, arguing that knowledge of self leads to knowledge of God: "Indeed, our very poverty better discloses the infinitude of benefits reposing in God. The miserable ruin into which the rebellion of the first man cast us, especially compels us to look upward" (I, 36). Presumably knowledge of the helpless wretchedness of man is essential to salvation. And one can perhaps see Lear as having reached this state of perception when he asks to wipe his hand, since it "smells of mortality." Furthermore, Hardin Craig has pointed out that the mere act of learning (and this would notably include learning about oneself) came with the Reformation to be considered "necessary for the hereafter as well as for the here and now. Men were suddenly made responsible for the achievement of their own salvation, not a salvation resting on virtue and obedience only, but resting also on comprehension." [17] To this extent, certainly, *King Lear* is a play showing the grim progress of an old man, through the agony of learning how wretched he and mankind are, toward redemption. But of course, as we have seen, it is not an explicitly Christian play; and Frye could argue that grace is lacking. To find it, we must join the allegorizers in finding Christ in Cordelia.

IX

We must not, of course, limit our interpretation of Lear's self-discovery to the treatises dealing with *nosce teipsum*. I would stress that these are not, except for Calvin (who belongs only partially in the genre), seminal works. They are highly derivative, most of their ideas being traceable to classical or medieval sources. They have, primarily, the virtue of embodying, in contemporary and conveniently available form, a set of ideas that the Renaissance chose to group together under the head of *nosce teipsum*. But there was doubtless a reason for the Renaissance need to

---

[17] *The Enchanted Glass* (Oxford: Basil Blackwell, 1950), p. 143.

formulate even a derivative theory about self-knowledge. It was an age when man, and notably individual man, was becoming increasingly self-conscious, more anxious concerning his identity. As a corporate order disintegrated, and the reassuring external limits upon his status became less firm, man had to look within himself for goals and controls. And it was also not unnatural that what was preeminently, even at times reluctantly, an age of discovery should, as the growing number of psychological works testify, find a challenging area for exploration within man himself.

Furthermore, these treatises on self-knowledge assist us in keeping our mind on certain substantial Renaissance contexts for the subject. Without them, for example, we might fail to see that, as a foremost student of Calvin has said, "Our knowledge of ourselves may be construed to include both all mankind and all creation (of which man is a microcosm)." [18] And without them we might fail to realize the immense importance the Renaissance student of self-knowledge put on the passions and, particularly, the body, with its necessities and frailties, and on the need for recognizing one's status as man rather than king or other proud creature. Most important, perhaps, they underline the current urgency of the subject in Shakespeare's day.

Nor are these treatises altogether lacking in subtle insights. There is a startlingly modern note, for example, in Charron's directions for the process of self-discovery. One acquires self-knowledge, he writes,

by a true, long and daily study of himselfe, a serious and attentive examination not only of his words, and actions, but of his most secret thoughts (their birth, progresse, continuance, repetition) and whatsoever is in him, even in his nightly dreames, prying and pinching him even to the quicke.

(p. 6)

Here, certainly, is an intimacy of self-examination worthy of the subtlety of psychoanalysis and justifying a search for no less an insight in Shakespeare's method for Lear. At the very least we can

---

[18] John T. McNeill in his edition of the *Institutes*, ed. cit., I, 37.

seek for Lear's "most secret thoughts (their birth, progresse, continuance, repetition)."

Again, even in the pedestrian verse of Sir John Davies we find a
perception that is not too unworthy of Shakespeare's lesser insights. Davies points out that man's soul "Doth of all sights his
own sight least endure":

> For even at first reflection she espies
> Such strange chimeras and such monsters there;
> Such toys, such antics, and such vanities,
> As he retires, and shrinks for shame and fear.

> (p. 348)

Modern psychology knows this only too well, but in the Renaissance, Shakespeare was one of the few who could grasp, as he did
in the person of Lear, the full horror, the "shame and fear," that
comes from seeing the "strange chimeras and such monsters" in
one's inmost nature and in those natures bred by one's own flesh.

X

But the reader, particularly if he is uneasy about a historical
approach to a work unparalleled in imaginative grandeur, may still
justifiably wish for a more precise vindication of these didactic
treatises. He may wish, for example, to know if, despite occasional
resemblances in idea, Shakespeare need have known the treatises
at all. As the present study, except for the last chapter, does not
make steady use of these works, it may be in order to point out
why I think Shakespeare had some knowledge of them, and to
suggest a Renaissance attitude toward them which may have impelled him to transmute their plain moral lessons to the highest
drama.

A major reason for believing that Shakespeare knew at least the
methodology of these books is that he uses the several "topics" for
self-discovery found in many of them. Nature as tutor is too obvious and pervasive a theme to need elaboration here, and moreover the subject of nature in King Lear has been well studied by

John F. Danby.[19] Another of the traditional "topics," the difficulty of acquiring self-knowledge, is exploited in more individual
fashion and in a way that lifts the treatment well above the broad
generalizations of the treatises. Shakespeare apparently did not
make the fall of man basic to this difficulty; instead he dramatized
the problem by taking a proud, inflexible, and unreflective old
man, to whom thought is uncongenial, and subjecting him
through a "tough World" to pressures that necessitate a change in
his habit of thought. I comment at some length upon this highly
dramatic device in the next chapter. Flattery as a deterrent to self-
discovery is more obvious, particularly in the opening scene. Affliction as a stimulus to self-discovery is superbly worked into the
dramatic action, and it is an affliction more specifically therapeutic
than the treatises would of themselves have suggested, except perhaps for the magnificent statement by Ralegh. Each agent of
agony for Lear—as for example his ineffectuality in the storm—
seems to awaken him to one of the several things about himself
which he must learn. And in the "specifics" of affliction for self-
discovery, there is a difference between those of the body, designed
for the sensualist Gloucester, and those of the mind applied to the
spiritually untried Lear. I have already suggested minimizing in interpretation the role of error in judgment, unless it is prompted by
passion. The treatises, we recall, are in their own limited way more
trustworthy than some modern critics in that they do not consider
recognition of error in judgment, taken by itself, to be a significant
part of self-discovery.

These "topics" are then all present in the play and point to the
possibility that Shakespeare had a more philosophical methodology
in reworking an unphilosophical group of plot sources into a
drama of self-discovery than meets the modern eye. What en-
courages me in this conviction is that there remain the two most
important "topics" of self-discovery, and these are basic to the play
and to the theme of this book. These are a study of one's passions
and a study of one's body. The second of these I take up in the
last chapter. But as the first of them, the study of one's passions, is

<hr>

[19] *Shakespeare's Doctrine of Nature: A Study of King Lear* (London: Faber
& Faber, Ltd., 1949).

not elsewhere consecutively discussed, I here briefly suggest ways in which Shakespeare has Lear learn about himself by both discovering and striving to master, often through comprehension, his passions.

At the beginning of the play Lear seems incapable of any emotion other than wrath ("Come not between the dragon and his wrath"). His pomp has not yet taken physic, and he cannot feel what mankind feels. A great deal of what he discovers about himself is the full range of emotion hidden beneath his stiff, pompous exterior, a range of emotion which, incredibly, proves to be wider than that of any other Shakespearean character with the possible exception of Hamlet. He learns, and not merely feels, that he is capable of "hot tears" for himself (I.iv.320), and then later that he is capable of a pity, which almost kills him, for himself as an exemplar of mankind (IV.vii.53–54). Still another emotion, a "sovereign shame" (IV.iv.44) and a "burning shame" (IV.iv.48), "elbows" him as he reflects upon the injustice he has done Cordelia.

The conscious experiencing of emotion is, however, only part of his self-discovery through knowledge of latent passion. In the manner prescribed by the *nosce teipsum* treatises, he struggles to control his emotions, and he does so because he comes to understand them. When hysterical sorrow afflicts him, he tries to master it:

> O, how this mother swells up toward my heart!
> Hysterica passio, down, thy climbing sorrow,
> Thy element's below!

> (*II.iv.36–38*)

And a little later:

> O me, my heart, my rising heart! But down.
> (*II.iv.122*)

His struggle to remain "patient," even when he is rapidly receiving blow after blow to his pride and very identity, is one of his most remarkable achievements. Exhausted and bewildered as he is refused admission to Gloucester's castle, he succeeds in checking his hysterical rage while he tries to analyze what may be the cause

of emotion in himself as well as the cause of heartlessness in
Regan and Cornwall:

> I'll forbear;
> And am fallen out with my more headier will,
> To take the indispos'd and sickly fit
> For the sound man.

> (II.iv.110–113)

Even during the intolerable provocation to rage during his quarrel
with Goneril and Regan at Gloucester's castle, he is capable of
studying his passion:

> I can be patient; I can stay here with Regan,
> I and my hundred knights,

> (II.iv.233–234)

though of course there is a querulous assertiveness in his insistence
on the knights. Presently, even though his control becomes more
precarious, he still fights for patience:

> You heavens, give me that patience, patience I need!
> (II.iv.274)

During the storm scene he alternately lashes out in anger at the
universe and resolves to "be the pattern of all patience" (III.ii.
37). He also grasps the hazard of his passions leading him to
insanity. First yielding to excruciating pity for himself ("Your old
kind father, whose frank heart gave you all"), he recognizes and at
least temporarily controls his progress through such emotion to
madness:

> O, that way madness lies; let me shun that,
> No more of that.

> (III.iv.19–20)

Perhaps most significantly of all, he does more than recognize
and try to control his grief. His study of his own passions takes a
more profound form as he recognizes some psychological truths
about their nature. Elsewhere [20] I have examined the way in

---

[20] "Hamlet's Therapy," *Huntington Library Quarterly*, XXVII (1964), 239–
258.

which the treatises such as we have surveyed, in addition to some
that are more purely psychological, anticipate modern conclusions,
reached first by Freud and then at greater length by Karl Men-
ninger, in proposing that pathological grief (notably in Hamlet)
may be merely a disguise for anger. As a remedy for grief, certain
moral and psychological treatises cautiously prescribed that its
concealed cause, anger, be given vent. Timothy Bright, one of the
most influential guides to a man's understanding himself through
his passions, wrote:

And if no other perswasion will serve a vehement passion, of another sort is to be kindeled, that may withdrawe that vain and
foolish sorowe into some other extremity, as of anger. . . . For
although they both breed a dislike, yet that proceedeth of other
cause, rebateth the force of it which gave first occasion, and as one
pinne is driven out with another, so the later may expell the
former. . . .[21]

The danger of "smothering" choler, if one is fighting madness, is
also expressed by Charron:

There are some that smother their choler within, to the end it
breake not forth, and that they may seem wise and moderate; but
they fret themselves inwardly, and offer themselves a greater violence than the matter is worth.

(p. 564)

That Shakespeare was aware of this view of the passions is evident
from Malcolm's advice to the mutely grief-stricken Macduff:

Be this the whetstone of your sword; let grief
Convert to anger; blunt not the heart, enrage it.
(Macbeth IV.iii.228-229)

Similarly Lear, who has found that mere control of grief and mere
patience are leading him to insanity, resolves to give expression to
the real emotion beneath the grief. Describing himself as a man
"As full of grief as age," he begs the gods not to "fool" him "so
much / To bear it tamely." Rather, he asks, "touch me with noble

---

[21] A Treatise of Melancholy (London, 1586), pp. 255-256.

anger" (II.iv.276–279). But though, like Hamlet and Macduff and far more magnificently than they, he does convert grief to anger, his mind is by this time unhinged. He has, nevertheless, remained sane long enough to have made a significant self-discovery, even under intolerable stress, of the true nature of his passions. That this leads to some of the greatest poetry and greatest drama in the play should not blind us to the prosaic theme of *nosce teipsum* running beneath the spectacle. And, as I attempt to show in chapter vi, this is equally true of his self-discovery in terms of man's body.

Still another question concerning the relationship of the pedestrian treatises to Shakespeare's imaginative masterpiece must be asked. Granted that Shakespeare may have followed their methodology, even to the extent of putting greatest stress upon the passions and the body, was he a sufficiently wide reader to have been likely to encounter such books, in which Lear is never mentioned, and to use them as even secondary sources? The recent researches of Kenneth Muir and Geoffrey Bullough have rendered old-fashioned the idea of Shakespeare as a limited reader. Muir in particular has dared to propose, and so far with a success approaching that of John Livingston Lowes on Coleridge, an extremely wide, though hurried, acquaintance of Shakespeare with the books of his time. For *King Lear* Muir cites, besides the innumerable possible sources for the plot, seven other works that might have shaped the texture or ideas of the play.[22] He concludes:

Shakespeare created King Lear from the most heterogeneous materials. As was his custom, he amplified and complicated his original fable by using incidents, ideas, phrases, and words from a variety of books. He found material for his purposes in the most unlikely places.[23]

Professor Muir does not investigate any of the treatises on *nosce teipsum* in his study of *King Lear*, but had he done so he probably would have sought them in "the most unlikely places." Aside from

[22] *King Lear*, ed. by Kenneth Muir (Arden Shakespeare; London: Methuen & Co., Ltd., 1952), pp. xlii–xliii.
[23] *Shakespeare's Sources: I. Comedies and Tragedies*, p. 162.

the evidence I have offered, however, it might be illuminating to see just how inconsiderable these works were in terms of reader appeal. One of the best guides we have for assessing this appeal is the number of editions through which a book went. I cite figures for only those works I consider it most likely from internal evidence that Shakespeare looked at. Boaistuau went through six editions in England; Sir John Davies and Thomas Wright, five editions; La Primaudaye, in English translations of the various versions of his book, nine editions; and Charron, though his publication in England was too late for Shakespeare to have used the work in translation except in manuscript, had five editions in English. At the very least these figures suggest that the books were available and conspicuous, and the subject very popular.

Finally, it may help to speculate what attitude Shakespeare, as a poetic rather than philosophical artist, might have taken toward the treatises of moral philosophers. Rolf Soellner, in an illuminating article defending Shakespeare's high opinion of the philosophers, points out that Renaissance humanists, of whose number Shakespeare in many ways was one,

> did not separate philosophy hermetically from literature and frequently identified philosophy with pleasingly expressed thought, Granted, they often thought and admired the commonplace. But we, in our latter-day sophistication, might well remind ourselves that the great and vital commonplaces on life, death, and immortality have all through the ages been illuminated by great philosophers.[24]

But, in general, Shakespeare is not reliably explicit about his literary theory and practice. Fortunately, however, two of his greatest poetic contemporaries, Sidney and Spenser, have left fairly clear accounts of what they felt about the relationship between the moral philosopher and the imaginative artist, and we may assume that Shakespeare's attitude was not radically different from theirs.

Although Sidney makes good-natured sport of the moral philosophers with their "sullen gravity," their angry treatises against

[24] " 'Hang up Philosophy!' Shakespeare and the Limits of Knowledge," *Modern Language Quarterly*, XXIII (1962), 148.

anger, and their colorless precepts, he recognizes their worth and their service as a basis from which the poet may proceed. Central to our purposes, he affirms "the knowledge of a mans selfe" to be "the highest end of the mistres Knowledge." [25] But even more important is his concept of how the poet can bring the moral doctrine to vivid life, with energeia. The poet "yeeldeth to the powers of the minde an image of that whereof the Philosopher bestoweth but a woordish description: which dooth neyther strike, pierce, nor possesse the sight of the soule so much as [poetry] doth" (p. 17). Then he cites examples, close to Shakespeare's method in *King Lear*, of how great poets have transmuted precepts into speaking pictures. Lily B. Campbell has argued that the poet was increasingly taking over the function of the historian (a profession also deprecated by Sidney), and it is likely that the poet was similarly finding increasingly valuable the works of the moral philosophers. [26]

Spenser's account, though briefer, is perhaps even more illuminating than Sidney's, for he gives it superb and deliberate illustration in his great epic. It is also significant that he finds it necessary to defend his fictional (or what he calls his "Allegoricall") approach against the customary philosophical one. Defending his imaginative procedure in *The Faerie Queene*, he writes in his letter to Sir Walter Ralegh:

> To some I know this Methode will seeme displeasaunt, which had rather have good discipline delivered plainly in way of precepts, or sermoned at large, as they use, then thus clowdily enwrapped in Allegoricall divises. But such, me seeme, should be satisfide with the use of these dayes, seeing all things accounted by their showes, and nothing esteemed of, that is not delightfull and pleasing to commune sense. . . . So much more profitable and gratious is doctrine by ensample, then by rule. [27]

[25] *An Apologie for Poetrie*, ed. by Evelyn S. Shuckburgh (Cambridge: The University Press, 1951), p. 13.

[26] *The Mirror for Magistrates*, ed. by Lily B. Campbell (Cambridge: The University Press, 1938), p. 51.

[27] *The Poetical Works of Edmund Spenser*, ed. by J. C. Smith and E. De Selincourt (London: Oxford University Press, 1950), p. 407.

Spenser seems to have been more sorely torn than was Shake-speare between the demands of the teaching and the delighting purposes of poetry. But though *The Faerie Queene* has a more pronounced moral purpose than any of Shakespeare's plays, and though the "doctrine by ensample" is not always so imaginatively disguised as in Shakespeare, the two poets were facing together the tastes and conventions of an age that wanted both the precepts and the "showes."

Spenser's knights, further, offer an interesting parallel to Shake-speare's Lear in that they are not perfected virtues, but errant, learning human beings in quest of the virtue that dominates the book in which each appears. The best parallel to *King Lear* (and not merely because the story of Lear is told in his book) is the tale of Sir Guyon, who, though seeking primarily Temperance, is fun-damentally engaged in a Renaissance quest for self-knowledge. His experiences and lessons fall under some of the "topics" treated in the books on *nosce teipsum*. He makes mistaken judgments, mainly as a result of passion; he wars with and studies passions, both his own and others'; and, in an entire canto, he learns about the human body. And where Lear has the guidance of Kent and the Fool, Guyon in his quest has the help of the Palmer. I would not, of course, push this parallel too far, though I am convinced that the dynamics of self-discovery in *The Faerie Queene* have been overlooked. For instance, when Guyon meets the blushing maiden Shamefastnesse, he himself blushes, and Alma has to ex-plain to him that his discomfiture at seeing the lady is really dis-comfiture at finding out a truth about himself (II.ix.43). Certainly the reader's intense absorption in the story is far more than that which comes from following a plot of knightly adventure. The reader is gripped, as in *King Lear*, by involvement with a character like Guyon as he comes to recognize the power of his concealed passions. And, like Shakespeare, Spenser has achieved some of his success by transmuting, though less totally, the lessons of the *nosce teipsum* treatises into poetry.

I think, as it should now be apparent, that these books were used by poets as great as Shakespeare and Spenser, and were cer-tainly known by Sidney. But, as I have said, it would too much limit an interpretation of *King Lear* to base an entire study of the play upon them. I value their existence and importance mainly in that they will help to control an approach to the play which would otherwise be too modern or, even worse, too subjective.

III
The Emergence
of Lear as Thinker

Renaissance clues to the substance of what Lear might be expected
to learn, even if Shakespeare made deliberate use of them, are not
enough grounds upon which to begin a broadly based analysis of
his self-discovery. We must also, for one thing, be aware of the
quality of his mind, its adaptability, persistence, and reasonableness. And we must inquire into the dramatic means whereby
Shakespeare depicts Lear as thinker, learning, discovering himself;
for, in a drama, one cannot estimate the quality of a mind without
taking into account the ways a mind reveals itself in dramatic action. It is easy enough to appreciate a Hamlet's intelligence in his
analytical soliloquies; it is difficult, but possibly more rewarding, to
see a Lear reluctantly, erratically, incoherently groping his way toward the truth. In contrast with other critics, I consider Lear one
of the high points of Shakespeare's interest in and development of
the tragic hero as thinker. And to appreciate and understand this
mental aspect of Lear, and the dramatic art behind it, we must
first make a survey of Shakespeare's earlier experiments of this
kind. We shall then see, I believe, that Lear, rather than Brutus or
Hamlet, is the most impressive depiction of a hero thinking his
way toward self-discovery.

II

Though not a play but a long narrative poem, *The Rape of
Lucrece* offered Shakespeare an early opportunity to depict a
nearly tragic character in the agony of introspection. No real self-
discovery results, except for a momentary revulsion of feeling
rather than thought after the dishonorable deed. But the leisurely
pace of the narrative before the rape, a high seriousness in the

poet, and a remarkable interest in the mind of an otherwise contemptible character produced Shakespeare's earliest prolonged inquiry into a character's thought. Tarquin debates the venture, as Macbeth was later to debate his. It is essentially a "To do, or not to do" kind of problem rather than the "Who am I?" kind to be explored in *King Lear*. In other words, it is a self-debate rather than a self-inquiry, and it explores alternatives rather than the nature of man.

Artistically it is interesting, for it not only embodies thoughtfulness and the mind at work; it supplies, as the later plays are to do, the dramatic context for the thought—almost, indeed, the stage business. Tarquin, upon retiring to his chamber, is said to

> lie revolving
> *The sundry dangers of his will's obtaining.*
> (ll. 127–128)

And, in the intense atmosphere of "the dead of night" whose only sounds are "owls' and wolves' death-boding cries," and stricken with the premeditated horror of the deed, Tarquin is described in a struggle of thought that might do credit to a later hero in soliloquy:

> *Here pale with fear he doth premeditate*
> *The dangers of his loathsome enterprise,*
> *And in his inward mind he doth debate*
> *What following sorrow may on this arise.*
> (ll. 183–186)

The "soliloquy" that follows—the debate "in his inward mind"— is dramatic and is an earnest of theatrical projection. It is marked, for example, by questions, some of them with the hopelessness of Macbeth's or Claudius'. And—another aspect auguring future psychological and dramatic insight—it ends with the abandonment of thought:

> *"Then, childish fear, avaunt! debating, die!*
> *Respect and reason, wait on wrinkled age!*
> *My heart shall never countermand my eye.*

> Sad pause and deep regard beseem the sage;
> My part is youth, and beats these from the stage."
>
> (ll. 274–278)

"Sad pause and deep regard" will come with Brutus. Here, as with Romeo, the youthful Tarquin impatiently gives up uncongenial thought. And probably one of the reasons that thinking is so slightly depicted in Shakespeare's early plays is that his protagonists are young men, in whom will conventionally prevails over reason.

III

This is, however, not true of Shakespeare's first tragedy, *Titus Andronicus*. Here we have, as in *King Lear*, an extremely old man. Furthermore, in his returning to "peace" in triumph and preparing to abandon the cares of life, he prefigures Lear's intent to "shake all cares and business from our age." For both men, of course, the "retirement" is to be merely the beginning of life's instruction. But, unlike Lear, Titus has very little capacity for thought. To be sure, he is late in the play shown in what is supposed to be meditation:

> Who doth molest my contemplation?
> Is it your trick to make me ope the door
> That so my sad decrees may fly away
> And all my study be to no effect?
>
> (V.ii.9–12)

Here are the stage properties of contemplation—Titus "opens his study door"—but he has been contemplating only the tactics of revenge. There has been no progress in insight, despite the most grotesque afflictions, since the beginning of the play. What intelligence he shows is the crafty madness of the antic Hamlet.

But in two respects his behavior suggests that it was devised by the same man, some fifteen years younger, who was to create *King Lear*. First, there is an imperious lack of reasonableness in the early scenes. Like Lear, Titus makes two disastrous decisions at the beginning of the play: the sacrifice of Alarbus and the endorsement of Saturninus as emperor. Both are made without much explanation, and there is a frightening ritualistic quality in the way he commands the sacrifice. Like Lear, he seems to have no give-and-take contact with other people. He does not argue; he scarcely seems to listen, let alone think. Second, again like Lear, he at last learns, "feelingly" but not thoughtfully, the experience of suffering. But his response is a lyrical kind of self-dramatization rather than any change in his attitude toward himself. He is sadder but not wiser. Nevertheless, the self-dramatization rather than the self-study is to become, and impressively so in *King Lear*, an important aspect of the way a tragic hero's mind reacts to adversity. When Titus sees the ravished and maimed Lavinia, his study is solely how to express his grief:

> Shall thy good uncle and thy brother Lucius
> And thou and I sit round about some fountain,
> Looking all downwards, to behold our cheeks
> How they are stain'd, like meadows yet not dry
> With miry slime left on them by a flood?
> And in the fountain shall we gaze so long
> Till the fresh taste be taken from that clearness,
> And made a brine-pit with our bitter tears?
>
> . . . .
>   Let us that have our tongues
> Plot some device of further misery,
> To make us wond'red at in time to come.
>
>   (III.i.222–135)

Here, to be sure, is a kind of self-study; but it is a study of oneself in the *attitude* of grief. And it has in addition a concern with the devising of stratagem—the stratagem of grief's depiction, the kind of tactical thinking that marks the later Titus and is the sole kind of which he becomes capable. Most important, however, throughout Shakespeare's delineation of his later tragic heroes there will be found a combat in the hero's reaction to suffering, a combat between the kind of thinking that goes into self-insight and the kind that produces self-pity and dramatization. Both kinds require acumen of a sort, and it is natural that Shakespeare as dramatist and actor would not only sympathize with the self-dramatizing kind of thought; he would depict it extraordinarily well as his art developed.

IV

In Shakespeare's next important tragedy, *Richard III*, the hero gives promise at the outset of being not only a very shrewd thinker but a character inclined to searching and honest self-examination. What is more, there is the necessary kind of affliction, in the form of a misshapen body, to have provided Shakespeare the materials for a tragic study similar in success to what Middleton and Rowley achieved in DeFlores. But, except for one fine scene near the conclusion, there is no advantage taken of Richard as a tragic hero of the sympathetic type—that is, if we regard a view of the hero's mind responding to affliction as indispensable to tragic effect.

Richard, to be sure, is a cerebral character, the most intelligent one Shakespeare had yet created. But the thinking he does is mainly that of detached amusement. He does not become thoughtfully engaged with experience, either his own or others', except of course in tactical planning. Most of his wit (and the term is more appropriate than "thought") is devoted to the *control* rather than the *understanding* of experience. For him man is a puppet to manipulate rather than to study; and this is true to a certain extent even of himself. He enjoys the antics into which he can force people and, as the desire for a looking glass suggests, he is even interested comically in himself as he is forced by a clever fate into becoming an object of mockery. When a character reaches a point where Richard's intelligence may not be able to manipulate him, Richard turns angrily from him. This occurs when Buckingham first resists Richard's control and threatens to show signs of reacting with thought to what Richard's wit had planned as his comic role. Upon Buckingham's hesitation about killing the princes, Richard remarks:

> *I will converse with iron-witted fools*
> *And unrespective boys; none are for me*
> *That look into me with considerate eyes.*
>
> (*IV.ii. 28–30*)

The last part of this speech is especially significant, for Richard here inadvertently reveals that he himself will resist looking inward "with considerate eyes." And a few lines later:

> *The deep-revolving witty Buckingham*
> *No more shall be the neighbour to my counsels.*
>
> (*IV.ii.42–43*)

Unlike Titus, Richard II, Hamlet, or Lear, Richard really has no adequately worthy antagonist, usually an antagonist of colder intelligence than his, to force him into anxious thought that might lead to self-discovery.

Only at the end of the play is Richard forced into such a situation, and here it is a sufficiently painful one to compel his full mind and not just his wit into activity. And the antagonist here is more profound than witty, although in the total irony of the play it is also that. The antagonist is providential retribution.

The moment of thought to which I refer is the most brilliant one that Shakespeare had yet devised. It is the soliloquy that follows Richard's awakening from his nightmare in which he has seen the ghosts of his victims. Notice that it begins with the atmosphere of stage effects, and that the whole speech is dramatic rather than expository.

> *O coward conscience, how dost thou afflict me!*
> *The lights burn blue. It is now dead midnight.*
> *Cold fearful drops stand on my trembling flesh.*
> *What! do I fear myself? There's none else by.*
> *Richard loves Richard; that is, I am I.*
> *Is there a murderer here? No. Yes, I am.*
> *Then fly. What, from myself? Great reason why,*

Lest I revenge. What, myself upon myself?
Alack, I love myself. Wherefore? For any good
That I myself have done unto myself?
O, no! alas, I rather hate myself
For hateful deeds committed by myself!
I am a villain: yet I lie, I am not.
Fool, of thyself speak well; fool, do not flatter.
My conscience hath a thousand several tongues,
And every tongue brings in a several tale,
And every tale condemns me for a villain.
Perjury, perjury, in the high'st degree;
Murder, stern murder, in the dir'st degree;
All several sins, all us'd in each degree,
Throng to the bar, crying all, Guilty! guilty!
I shall despair. There is no creature loves me,
And if I die no soul shall pity me.

(V.iii.179–201)

The speech has merited quoting at length because it so well dis-
plays Shakespeare's early experiment with the kind of thinking
that leads to self-discovery, even though it seems, in comparison
with *King Lear*, tacked on to the play, whereas in *King Lear* the
thoughtful recognition is distributed, at dramatic moments,
throughout most of the action. Here, at any rate, we find Richard's
fullest reasoning power engaged, because he is arguing with the
only human adversary in the play whose intelligence is equal to his
own—himself. In this self-debating, however, the passage is in the
tradition of Brutus, Hamlet, and Claudius rather than Lear. That
aspect of the soliloquy which is in the manner of Lear is its hysterical incoherence, the dramatic rather than the systematic process
of thought. Equally important is the fundamental reason for the
nervous urgency of the thought. Richard for the first time is questioning his own identity:

What! do I fear myself? There's none else by.
Richard loves Richard; that is, I am I.
Is there a murderer here? No. Yes, I am.
Then fly. What, from myself?

The hated and despised opposition, which Richard had hitherto regarded as external, is now seen as within him. What he sees makes him want to fly himself. Also important to our consideration of Lear is Richard's recognition that he needs love—a fact about himself which he had perceived only with witty scorn in his opening soliloquy. Proud reliance on his own wit has been proved —partly by that wit and partly by an emotional state—to be an inadequate way of life.

V

Richard II marks still another stage in Shakespeare's developing interest in the protagonist as thinker. This weak, proud monarch lacks the tough kind of intelligence of the earlier Richard. In fact, for much of the play we are inclined to regard him as either stupidly and petulantly imperious or sentimentally soft of mind. Yet he is closer to both Hamlet and Lear than is Richard III. Indeed, *Richard II* might be regarded as the point in Shakespeare's career when he first began to recognize the value of the protagonist as thinker—this despite the fact that the thinking is often mistaken and leads to very little accurate self-discovery.

The opening scenes parallel *Titus Andronicus* in their substitution of imperious ritual for thought. Richard, in stopping the combat and in banishing Bolingbroke and Aumerle, scarcely engages or even interests himself in what is going on. For most of the play he seems to be out of contact with a world where reasoning, discussion, and argument (including argument with oneself) are necessary. After York's long, passionate speech detailing Richard's misdeeds and his falling off from the family honor, Richard seems not to have heard him. He says only, "Why, uncle, what's the matter?" (II.i.186). And after York has elaborated still further on Richard's wrongdoings, especially the seizing of the dead Gaunt's property, the King replies, with no recognition of the argument that might have led him to see his true responsibilities as king and thereby avert his tragedy:

> *Think what you will, we seize into our hands*
> *His plate, his goods, his money, and his lands.*
>
> (*II.i.209–210*)

Presumably there is some thought going on in Richard's mind—
we see later that he can be more thoughtful than any previous
protagonist—but it is not expressed. Thought that is going on
without being expressed will prove in *King Lear* to be one of the
most dramatic kinds. But for the first part of the play there seems
to be little indication of such a dramatic purpose. Rather, Richard
impresses us as a king who has never had to justify his actions, to
others or to himself. Unless we take this view we are left with the
less satisfactory alternative that Shakespeare was characterizing
him carelessly, without interest enough in him to show his mind at
work.

At any rate, it is clear that midway through the play Richard
begins to think. The scene of Richard's return from Ireland
(III.ii) marks the point at which most of us become interested in
the play. Significantly, it also marks the point at which we begin to
see Richard in adversity. Stripped of his authority, forced to submit to humiliating bargaining with Bolingbroke, losing the identity of even his name, he provides an imperfect, but nevertheless
suggestive, model of what Shakespeare will create on a grander
scale in *King Lear*. But there is one all-important difference. Lear
engages in real thought and fights self-pity; Richard resists realistic
thought, indulges in self-pity, and turns all of his by no means
contemptible intelligence upon self-dramatization.

Richard's thinking takes at first the forms of prayers, laments,
and imprecations on his enemies. And it is dramatized by his
kneeling on the earth and then sitting on the earth as he indulges
in his famous "talk of graves, of worms, and epitaphs" (III.ii.145).
There is still at this point no contact with reality. When he reasons, it is rationalization of a self-pitying kind that seems to give
him as much satisfaction in being superior to events as Richard
III's more realistic kind of thought gave him. He reasons typically:

Say, is my kingdom lost? Why, 'twas my care;
And what loss is it to be rid of care?
Strives Bolingbroke to be as great as we?
Greater he shall not be: if he serve God,
We'll serve Him too and be his fellow so.
Revolt our subjects? That we cannot mend;
They break their faith to God as well as us.

(*III.ii.95–101*)

Obviously, as with Richard III, this is no more than virtuoso thought; but, unlike Richard III's, it does not even have the merit of practicality. Richard is reasoning himself off his throne.

For Richard's intelligence leads him almost invariably to wrong conclusions, about what course of action to take and about the cause of his downfall. The unintelligent choice of action is only too apparent throughout the first part, and the audience can see with conviction the real cause of his tragedy. But, as we have noted, there is no apparent thought behind these mistaken decisions. When the thought comes in the third act, it is largely an incorrect explanation for his tragedy. It makes him his own tragic chorus—an eloquent but an unreliable one. Never, perhaps, did Shakespeare depict misguided thinking more attractively.

In Richard's mind, he is a Christ figure betrayed by Judases; he is a victim of Fortune's wheel; and, though this is a little closer to the truth, he is one who wasted time and now in turn is wasted by time. His talk about the "sad stories of the death of kings" is, admittedly, at least temporarily persuasive and is also as close as he comes to what the Renaissance would consider self-knowledge. He sees the frailty, the unwarranted pomp of kings. "Mock not flesh and blood" is surely a fine Renaissance insight.

Also impressively approaching true insight are the two passages wherein Richard explicitly looks at himself. The superior is the first. In the process of pitying himself and blaming others for his fall, he has a sudden reversal of direction in his thought—not a radical one, for his self-image is still pompous, but enough to show that his thought can now change in midcareer:

> Mine eyes are full of tears, I cannot see;
> And yet salt water blinds them not so much
> But they can see a sort of traitors here.
> Nay, if I turn mine eyes upon myself,
> I find myself a traitor with the rest;
> For I have given here my soul's consent
> To undeck the pompous body of a king,
> Made glory base, a sovereignty a slave,
> Proud majesty a subject, state a peasant.
>
> (IV.i.244–252)

In the second episode of explicitly indicated self-study, he calls for a looking glass:

> I'll read enough,
> When I do see the very book indeed
> Where all my sins are writ, and that's myself.
> *Re-enter Attendant, with a glass.*
> Give me that glass, and therein will I read.
> No deeper wrinkles yet? Hath sorrow struck
> So many blows upon this face of mine,
> And made no deeper wounds? O flatt'ring glass,
> Like to my followers in prosperity,
> Thou dost beguile me!
>
> (IV.i.273–281)

But aside from the book wherein all his sins are written, this is not a profound reflection upon himself. The glass is "flatt'ring" only because it does not show his wrinkles. It beguiles him because it does show the face of the man who once was so powerful and wealthy. It is characteristic of Richard's self-study that it should be made in a mirror, not with analytical thought. And it is further posed in its control. A Hamlet and a Lear will reveal "excitements" in their thoughts. There will be high drama in the nervous, incoherent moments of their insights.

Nevertheless, there is more thought in this play than in any preceding tragedy. What is more, Shakespeare uses devices and tricks to make Richard *seem* a thinker, though there is no attempt to deceive the audience into the conviction that he is an impressive one. The "sad stories" episode is not fully an augury of thoughtfulness; it has just a faint air of the ridiculous. Richard's sitting on the ground is simply one of a series of actions wherein he has alternately sat on the ground and then risen. The action, besides its suggestion of a jack-in-the-box, is still too suggestive of Richard's childish whims and sudden impulses.

Doubtless Richard's finest bit of stage business underlining pensiveness is the scene in prison in Pomfret Castle. This begins most promisingly:

> I have been studying how I may compare
> This prison where I live unto the world;
> And for because the world is populous
> And here is not a creature but myself,
> I cannot do it; yet I'll hammer it out.
> My brain I'll prove the female to my soul,
> My soul the father; and these two beget
> A generation of still-breeding thoughts,
> And these same thoughts people this little world,
> In humours like the people of this world.
> For no thought is contented.
>
> (V.v.1–11)

This passage is rich in the machinery of cerebration. There is much talk of thinking. But the total speech is not intellectually impressive. It is again virtuoso: the mental exercise of a man who is not closely engaged with his environment or even his own fate —let alone his identity. What makes the speech important as a milestone on the road to *King Lear* is that it does show, or at least gives the impression of showing, a man trying hard to think. Possibly Shakespeare himself did not know at this time how to make the *substance* of the thought, particularly as it leads to self-discovery, significant and probing. On the other hand, we must not discount the possibility that Richard as a self-conscious, but superficial, thinker was very much a part of Shakespeare's intention.

VI

With Brutus in *Julius Caesar* we come to the stage in Shakespeare's development where it is usually assumed that he began to concentrate upon the tragic hero as thinker. Certainly no earlier character is so *professionally* a thinker as Brutus. And certainly too the substance of his thinking is a major advance upon Richard II's. Notwithstanding, Brutus is in many ways not remarkably different from Richard, but represents as thinker simply an improvement upon the dramatic strategies Shakespeare had used in the earlier play.

For one thing there is in Brutus a prominently ritualistic aspect, well noticed by Brents Stirling.[1] Stirling's point is that Brutus makes his ugly deeds seem less repulsive by giving them the form of ritual. He will not face reality any more than Richard will. The same point might be made about his argumentation. His speech explaining the assassination is the most pronounced example of his failure—perhaps here a willful one—to face the honest facts and instead to gloss over ugliness by illogical appeals such as "Who is here so rude that would not be a Roman?" (III.ii.32–33). Further, there is the kind of ritualistic unreason, noticed as early as Titus, in his arguments with the conspirators. The main difference is that whereas Titus and Richard have an elevation of station that permits them not to listen to reason, Brutus' abstraction from realistic argument is seen as an aloofness of character, an idealism that need scarcely defend itself against argument.

Despite the fact that Brutus' mind seldom really descends into the arena of competitive thought, it has acquired a high reputation among critics. But this reputation cannot be based on any accuracy of judgment shown by Brutus. Like Titus and Richard II, he is a splendid example of one who makes the most glaring of mistakes. In every detail on which he calmly overrules the conspirators at their first meeting, he is wrong. He is later wrong when he insists

[1] " 'Or Else Were This a Savage Spectacle,' " *Unity in Shakespearian Tragedy* (New York: Columbia University Press, 1956), pp. 40–54.

that Antony be allowed to speak a funeral oration. And he is wrong when he prevails upon Cassius to join battle immediately. But Brutus is affectionately regarded by most readers as a thinker. Perhaps it is because of his soliloquies, rightly seen as foreshadowing Hamlet's. The most famous is of course that one beginning:

> *It must be by his death; and for my part,*
> *I know no personal cause to spurn at him*
> *But for the general. He would be crown'd:*
> *How that might change his nature, there's the question.*
> *(II.i.10–13)*

Virgil Whitaker has interestingly argued that this soliloquy is shot through with fallacious logic, an intentional and significant stroke on Shakespeare's part.[2] There is plausibility in this contention, for not only were Elizabethan audiences alert to formal logic, but elsewhere in his thinking Brutus is impulsive rather than logical. On the other hand, it is also clear, in "there's the question," that Shakespeare is here on the road to Hamlet's great soliloquy. What, at any rate, is significant about Brutus' faulty thinking—especially in terms of how Shakespeare is preparing for Lear—is that Shakespeare early found, even in his most pensive character, that erratic thinking can be as effective a dramatic device as profound and systematic thinking. Indeed, good dramatic use can be made of the very absence of thought. Both can be useful in depicting the drama of self-discovery. On the stage, as on the couch, man seldom *reasons* his way toward insight.

But what has really given Brutus his reputation as a thinker is something that can be found to a lesser extent in *Richard II*: he is frequently seen in thought and he is given the posture, or what might better be called the costume, of a thinker. There are several references to his insomnia. This is a mild symptom of thought compared with the utter exhaustion and madness that Lear as thinker will endure; but it for a time seems with Shakespeare a

[2] *Shakespeare's Use of Learning: An Inquiry into the Growth of his Mind & Art* (San Marino, Calif.: Huntington Library, 1953), pp. 242–245.

favorite costume for a thinking protagonist. The most famous of the references to Brutus' insomnia is characteristically his own:

> Since Cassius first did whet me against Caesar,
> I have not slept.
>
> (II.i.61–62)

And the second is also by Brutus:

> Boy! Lucius! Fast asleep? It is no matter;
> Enjoy the honey-heavy dew of slumber.
> Thou hast no figures nor no fantasies
> Which busy care draws in the brains of men;
> Therefore thou sleep'st so sound.
>
> (II.i.229–233)

And there is the beautiful scene (IV.iii) before Philippi when Brutus' servant falls asleep playing for his master. This scene is also embellished by another part of the thinker's costume, a book. And Brutus is twice referred to as meditating. The more moving instance is when he is contemplating his death, as Dardanius remarks, "Look, he meditates" (V.v.12). Surely all this is not intended merely to show Brutus as a poseur. Shakespeare is genuinely becoming interested in a hero as thinker, but he is at the same time aware that there is a more interesting characterization possible if there are contradictions.

Brutus must, despite his obvious mental flaws and his self-dramatization, be regarded as an intellectual. What is then remarkable is that this thinking hero makes less self-discovery than does Lear. Near the beginning of the play there are two hints that Shakespeare may be intending to make Brutus a hero who achieves anagnorisis. Brutus tells Cassius:

> If I have veil'd my look,
> I turn the trouble of my countenance
> Merely upon myself.
>
> (I.ii.37–39)

And a few lines further he asks:

> Into what dangers would you lead me, Cassius,
> That you would have me seek into myself
> For that which is not in me?
>
> (I.ii.63–65)

There is irony in the last speech, though possibly Shakespeare did not intend it. There would have been, indeed, the greatest of danger for Brutus' ego if he had truly looked within himself. But Brutus never, I believe, comes close to self-discovery, or even to a truth of any kind. His final speech is self-congratulatory, particularly the following part of it:

> Countrymen,
> My heart doth joy that yet in all my life
> I found no man but he was true to me.
> I shall have glory by this losing day
> More than Octavius and Mark Antony
> By this vile conquest shall attain unto.
>
> (V.v.33–38)

The intellectual drama of Shakespeare's first impressively intellectual hero did not, therefore, turn out to be one of self-discovery. Brutus' mind was not, despite his pensive bent, essentially an introspective one. What he inquired of himself was mainly "To do, or not to do?" This limitation of the play is unfortunate for the development of Brutus into a major character, but not for the play as a whole. The play, with its political message, demands a limited role and an imperfect mind for a limited hero. Further, there would have been much less of interest to discover in the mind of Brutus than in that of Lear.

VII

Brutus' major importance is probably that he helped prepare Shakespeare for the creation of Hamlet, his most intelligent and intellectual hero. It would be both irrelevant and impossible here to try to do justice to the incomparably agile, inquisitive, and alert mind of Hamlet. But though Hamlet is radically different as a thinker from Lear, he is different in a significant way. We cannot appreciate Shakespeare's depiction of Lear's mentality without at least briefly studying his depiction of Hamlet's. What we can do is to see how Hamlet both differs from and carries on, as thinker, some of the traits we have seen in earlier heroes and also notice the innovations that either prepare for Lear or offer a significant contrast.

First, except for his crafty manner in revenge, there is little to recall Titus Andronicus. Nor is there the ritualistic quality—the absence of thoughtful contact with people and event in reasoning —that we found in Titus, Richard II, or Brutus. There is none of the earlier aloofness from problems, but rather an intense and interested involvement in all of them. And, above all, there is real intelligence. Hamlet indeed makes mistakes out of rashness and occasional abandonment of thought, but these, especially toward the end of the play, are generally to be interpreted as a relaxing of his own will and cunning in order to allow Providence to work. But of course his intelligence is not seen mainly in strategic or practical decisions.

There are, however, continuing traits. With Richard III, Hamlet shares a witty, satirical view of life. Like Richard, too, he enjoys manipulating people. His mind needs to be in control of his environment. One thinks of his pleasure in humiliating Polonius and Osric, his outwitting Rosencrantz and Guildenstern, and his supreme, hysterical pleasure in catching Claudius in the Mouse Trap. But unlike Richard, he seems to study and understand the people he manipulates. In his approach to humanity he is not merely a dramatist but a student.

It is with Richard II and particularly Brutus, of course, that Hamlet has the strongest ties. In a sense they are all "thinkers" as earlier heroes were not. In the most superficial sense they all have the costume of thinkers. Hamlet has the soliloquies, the solitude, the book; and there are many references to his pensiveness: "the pale cast of thought," "thinking too precisely on th'event," "A thought which, quarter'd," " 'Twere to consider too curiously to consider so."

But Hamlet is a genuinely searching kind of thinker. Unlike Richard II and Brutus, he does not impress us as self-consciously thoughtful; he is less interested in the posture of thought than in its object. He reflects upon suicide, the hereafter, morality, revenge, honor, action, guilt—to name but a few topics. And there are, for almost the first time in Shakespeare, reflections upon a few of the topics the Renaissance considered proper subjects for self-knowledge: the nature of man and woman, the body and its corruption, and sin.

These concerns are somewhat limited in the play, for *Hamlet* is not primarily a drama of self-discovery.[3] Though there is a question of identity in "To be, or not to be," the real concern is "To do, or not to do?" Hamlet achieves some insight into his corrupt nature in speeches like "O, what a rogue and peasant slave am I!" but here he is berating himself for not taking revengeful action. And when he tells Ophelia, "I am myself indifferent honest, but yet I could accuse me of such things that it were better my mother had not borne me" (III.i.123–125), he is probably most interested in frightening Ophelia (and possibly Claudius). There is little

---

[3] See, however, for a more complex view, probing into the nature of tragedy, Robert B. Heilman, "To Know Himself: An Aspect of Tragic Structure," *Review of English Literature*, V (1964), 36–57. Professor Heilman, tracing the development of the hero's self-knowledge from *Titus Andronicus* through *Hamlet*, makes continued use of the "duel" motif, the substitution of a war with others for a war with oneself: "What the tragic hero must come to know is that he was not innocent; it is by that movement that tragedy becomes the vehicle of the morall enlightenment appropriate to art" (p. 54). Hamlet so passionately desires innocence that he does not go far enough into true self-inquiry. The play only opens the door to the subsequent tragedies. Though my subject in this chapter is not self-knowledge primarily, and though Heilman's opinion of self-knowledge differs from mine, we seem to agree on the extent to which the various heroes are capable of self-knowledge. See also Barbara Burge, " 'Hamlet': The Search for Identity," *ibid.*, pp. 58–71. From a psychoanalytical point of view Hamlet may be said to discover himself when he gives expression to the anger beneath his melancholia, as I suggest in an article already referred to: "Hamlet's Therapy," *Huntington Library Quarterly*, XXVII (1964), 239–258.

contriteness in his catalogue of his sins: "I am very proud, revengeful, ambitious" (III.i.126). Hamlet does not so much need to learn about himself as about the corrupt world in which he lives.

The way in which *Hamlet* serves, as had no earlier play, as preparation for the depiction of thought in *King Lear* is in the way thinking is made intensely dramatic. There is a kind of muted drama in the sober meditations of a Brutus, or the controlled, witty intelligence of Gloucester's opening soliloquy. But what *Hamlet* provides is the passionate, often incoherent, thought of the kind that we have seen before, and then briefly, only in the panicky soliloquy of Richard after his nightmare. Hamlet's mind is rightfully regarded as a fine one, and its reasoning power is considerable. But we seldom see his mind calmly at work. The "To be, or not to be" soliloquy is probably well enough reasoned, though some critics have debated its logical progression.[4] But the powerful "O, what a rogue and peasant slave am I!" soliloquy shows his mind working under feverous urgency (what he calls "Excitements of my reason") and incoherently. There are hiatuses, and he jumps illogically from one subject to another, finally excitedly discovering a tactic that in fact he had discovered earlier.

It is not the accuracy and normalcy of Hamlet's thinking, but the painful gropings of his "distracted globe" then, which are the real innovations of the play for our purposes. In addition there is the near madness and the inspired byways along which it takes him in the morbid concern with death, with sex—all foreshadowing the larger number of illogical excursions to which Lear's madness will direct him. In other words, and to change the metaphor, the orchestration of thought in *Hamlet* is what is new; it is even more impressive than the content of the thought. Never before in English drama had a character's mind ranged with such antic grotesqueness, with such reason in madness, with such accurate irrelevancies.

---

[4] The most substantial recent study of the subject is Alex Newell, "The Dramatic Context and Meaning of Hamlet's 'To be or not to be' Soliloquy," *PMLA*, LXXX (1965), 38–50.

VIII

Despite the occasional wildness of his thought, Hamlet is rightly famous as an intellectual hero. Like Brutus, but on a much superior scale, Hamlet provided Shakespeare with a kind of satisfaction that he must have relished: a hero intelligent and articulate enough to permit him to comment meaningfully upon his own tragedy. It is therefore puzzling to see Shakespeare turn next to a tragic hero whom critics agree in seeing as a strong and impressive, but not a thoughtful, man.[5] For Othello can express only lyrically the agony of his plight. He is not intellectually equipped to enlarge by his own sense of tragedy upon man's plight in general; and it is particularly questionable whether he has a mind capable of self-discovery, or even knows accurately at the end of the play what has happened to him.[6]

In view of these probable limitations in Othello, it is paradoxical that the play concentrates upon thinking, and especially the problem of thinking, almost more than any previous one except *Hamlet*. The significant word most frequently used (even more frequently than *honest*) is *think* or *thought*. In one form or another *think* occurs eighty-four times in the play. A similar, but contrasting word, *know*, is used twenty-five times through the first scene of the third act, mainly by Othello. Thereafter, it is used hardly at all, being supplanted in the mouths of both Othello and Iago by the word *think*. In fact, the intellectual progress of Othello may be

[5] My comments on Othello as thinker are based on my article " 'Perplex'd in the Extreme': The Role of Thought in *Othello*," *Shakespeare 400: Essays by American Scholars on the Anniversary of the Poet's Birth*, ed. by James G. McManaway (New York: Holt, Rinehart and Winston, Inc., 1964), pp. 265–275.

[6] T. S. Eliot believes that he does not, that in his final speech he is taking (perhaps like Brutus?) an interpretation of his tragedy designed to comfort him. "Shakespeare and the Stoicism of Seneca," *Selected Essays of T. S. Eliot* (London: Faber & Faber, Ltd., 1951), pp. 130–131. For an unconvincingly low appraisal of Othello's intelligence, see Albert Gerard, " 'Egregiously an Ass': The Dark Side of the Moor. A View of Othello's Mind," *Shakespeare Survey* 10 (1957), pp. 99–100.

seen as a painful advance from knowing to a distorted form of thinking, then back to a hardened form of knowing.

Othello's native state of thought, that which has secured for him "the tranquil mind," is that of intuitive knowing rather than thinking. On the other hand, it does not seem to be a kind of knowing that can withstand for too long the agile antics of a "thinking" Iago. Nor is it the kind of trustworthy knowledge that can avert mental chaos when he is exposed to new evidence about himself and others. There is irony in the fact that Othello regards himself as highly competent in mind. In expressing his scornful rejection of the idea that love may make him dote, he affirms his belief in the value of his intellect:

> No, when light-wing'd toys
> Of feather'd Cupid seal with wanton dullness
> My speculative and offic'd instruments
> That my disports corrupt and taint my business,
> Let housewives make a skillet of my helm. . . .
>
> (I.iii.269–273)

This, and his earlier speeches before the Senate, are the firm, assured, massive utterances of a mind that is adequate as long as it does not have to shift from its orientation, from what it "knows." It is also significant that besides his addiction to *know*, Othello's vocabulary for his own mental activity suggests emotional rather than intellectual apprehension. One short speech in the first scene of Act II contains the following expressions: "wonder" (l. 185), "soul's joy" (l. 186), "fear" (l. 192), "this content" (l. 198), and "too much of joy" (l. 199).

By contrast, it is Iago who is depicted—or rather self-depicted—as the "thinking man" of the play. His are the plotting and analytical soliloquies. It is he, rather than the tragic hero, who has the costume of thought. He describes his intense concentration:

> I am about it; but indeed my invention
> Comes from my pate as birdlime does from frieze;
> It plucks out brains and all.
>
> (II.i.126–128)

Another graphic clue to Iago as a posing thinker comes from Othello in the temptation scene:

> And when I told thee he was of my counsel
> In my whole course of wooing, thou criedst, "Indeed!"
> And didst contract and purse thy brow together,
> As if thou then hadst shut up in thy brain
> Some horrible conceit. If thou dost love me,
> Show me thy thought.

(III.iii.111–116)

It is Iago who impresses Othello as "wise" and by his thoughtful pose—that of agonized thinking [7]—starts Othello on his excruciating pilgrimage of genuine but imperfect thought. The particular ordeal for Othello is that he cannot stand indecision; and indecision, at least in drama of moral choice, is the very essence of real thought:

> By the world,
> I think my wife be honest and think she is not.
> I think that thou art just and think thou art not.
> . . . .
> I'll not endure it. Would I were satisfied!

(III.iii.383–390)

A Hamlet in this dilemma would not be too uncomfortable; he seems even to relish intellectually some of his self-debates. But Othello cannot endure the uncongenial career of thought on which he has been launched, and in fact it lasts for scarcely more than one scene (III.iii). At the end of this scene his mind is made up. He reverts to "knowing," and as he does so, in the great Pontic Sea speech, he becomes the ritualist in a manner more frightening than that of Titus or Brutus. This is especially pronounced in his terrifyingly ritualistic manner in the murder scene, where he

---

[7] A stimulating case for the genuine, neurotically based agony of Iago's thought has been made by Marvin Rosenberg, *The Masks of Othello* (Berkeley and Los Angeles: University of California Press, 1961). See particularly pp. 176–178.

moves as in a trance, impervious to Desdemona's pleas and unwilling to reembark upon thinking.

Othello, then, is by no means a play lacking in thought. It is indeed more accurate to say that, next to *Hamlet*, it is the best depiction of thought that Shakespeare had as yet achieved. In *Hamlet*, Shakespeare had said most of what he had to say about an intellectual with a brilliant and agile mind. Even in that play, of course, Shakespeare shows the mind impeded, clouded, and agitated so that the thought is highly dramatic. But *Othello* is still something quite different. In this play we have an almost equally dramatic depiction of thought, at least in one great scene, in the person of a man for whom thinking is an agony, who has never had to question the honesty of man or his own nature. The resultant thought is but slightly shown in the form of soliloquies, for these represent the controlled working of his mind, the "knowing." The real thinking is depicted in increasingly uneasy dialogue, with progression of thought often only suggested beneath the surface: "O misery!" (III.iii.171); "And yet, how nature erring from itself,—" (III.iii.227); "No, not much mov'd. / I do not think but Desdemona's honest" (III.iii.224–225).

One can, at any rate, see that Othello as thinker is in the immediate path of advance to Lear as thinker. Both are shown first as resistant to thought; both have been unprepared by profession and circumstances for flexible or humble reflection; neither has had to question his own identity. In *King Lear* Shakespeare will choose for his hero the man least likely, from all appearances, to respond constructively to pressures necessitating thought and reevaluation of self. But the dramatist will have at his beck previous instructive experiments on how, with most dramatic effect, to show a character in the ordeal of thought.

IX

Regardless of how well prepared Shakespeare may have been to depict a chronic nonthinker as thinking hero, all his resources of dramaturgy would have been worthless if the hero were constitutionally incapable of significant thought. *Othello* was about as far as Shakespeare could go, in a major tragedy, with a hero of not conspicuously flexible and introspective intelligence. To a few critics, of whom G. Wilson Knight is the most eloquent spokesman, Lear is not an intelligent man. Knight writes of Lear:

A tremendous soul is, as it were, incongruously geared to a puerile intellect. . . . This, then, is the basis of the play: greatness linked to puerility. Lear's instincts are themselves grand, heroic—noble even. His judgement is nothing. He understands neither himself nor his daughters. . . . Lear starts his own tragedy by a foolish misjudgement. Lear's fault is a fault of the mind, a mind unwarrantably, because selfishly, foolish.[8]

Knight makes a valid point in contrasting the judgment and the soul. Lear has always impressed audiences more by his grandeur than by his acumen. But it will be part of my concern in the remainder of this book to show that Lear is not so contemptible in intellect as Knight and others have felt.

It is, at any rate, reassuring to observe that a handful of critics have made a more charitable appraisal of Lear's intelligence. Hazlitt acknowledges the unwieldy and towering build of Lear's mind, but correctly affirms its fundamental control. His use of a ship image is apt:

The mind of Lear, staggering between the weight of attachment and the hurried movements of passion, is like a tall ship driven about by the winds, buffeted by the furious waves, but that still rides above the storm, having its anchor fixed in the bottom of the sea.[9]

Francis G. Schoff has recently defended even Lear's practical wisdom. He contends that the play offers no evidence "in its lines" that Lear errs in disowning Cordelia or in dividing the kingdom

[8] "*King Lear* and the Comedy of the Grotesque," in *The Wheel of Fire: Interpretations of Shakespearean Tragedy, With Three New Essays* (Cleveland and New York: World Publishing Company [1957]; originally published 1930), p. 162.
[9] William Hazlitt, *The Round Table and Characters of Shakespear's Plays* (London: J. M. Dent & Sons, Ltd., 1944), p. 258.

and resigning power. Lear, according to Schoff, is neither stupid nor senile; only Goneril and Regan think so. And specific examples of Lear's astuteness are pointed out, including Lear's quick awareness of the quality of Kent in disguise, his noticing the slackening of services from Goneril and his servants, his admission of unfairness to Cordelia, and his acknowledgment that the fault may be his in being oversensitive.[10] But it is unlikely that Shakespeare intended so total a vindication of Lear's practical astuteness. There are plenty of mistakes, though not necessarily acts of stupidity, in what Lear does. Lear may be wise without being astute.

Probably the finest and most sympathetic description of Lear's mentality is that by Charles Lamb, though it comes unfortunately in the notorious context of pronouncing *King Lear* unfit for the stage:

The greatness of Lear is not in corporal dimensions, but in intellectual: the explosions of his passion are terrible as a volcano; they are storms turning up and disclosing to the bottom that sea, his mind, with all its vast riches. It is his mind which is laid bare. This case of flesh and blood seems too insignificant to be thought on; even as he himself neglects it. On the stage we see nothing but corporal infirmities and weakness, the impotence of rage; while we read it, we see not Lear, but we are Lear,—we are in his mind, we are sustained by a grandeur which baffles the malice of daughters and storms; in the aberrations of his reason, we discover a mighty irregular power of reasoning, immethodized from the ordinary purposes of life, but exerting its powers, as the wind blows where it listeth, at will upon the corruptions and abuses of mankind.[11]

For Shakespeare's achievement in depicting Lear as thinker, no better expression could be found than "a mighty irregular power of reasoning." Lamb has perceptively seen the wedding of grandeur and old but still strong intellect in the person of Lear. But Lamb's view is defective in failing to recognize the part that great per-

[10] "King Lear: Moral Example or Tragic Protagonist," *Shakespeare Quarterly*, XIII (1962), 159–162.

[11] *The Complete Works and Letters of Charles Lamb* (New York: Modern Library, 1935), pp. 298–299.

formance could have upon the *depiction* of Lear at thought. If it is Lear's "mind which is laid bare," that process must be rendered with all the stage effects that Shakespeare had learned up to this time; and even these will prove insufficient. There must be *displayed* the baffled, helpless groping for thought, the desperate fighting for reason and sanity, the hiatuses when the thinking is going on but is not expressed in words, the angry incoherence— and many more such effects. But Lamb no doubt saw these in his own mind, for "immethodized" is the word for the thinking process represented in *King Lear*.

At the beginning of the play Lear's mind is more rigid than either Titus' or Richard II's. No other hero seems less apt for the kind of adaptable thought that can lead to self-discovery. He makes also the unpromising announcement that in giving up his kingdom,

> '*tis our fast intent*
> *To shake all cares and business from our age. . . .*
>
> (*I.i.39–40*)

This implies that he is content with what he has achieved and become, and that he is retiring from a thoughtful concern with all of life.

But what immediately strikes us *dramatically* is the ritualistic unreasonableness, noted in less impressive form in the early heroes.[12] Here we have, not a reasonable explanation of action, but a "*Know* that we have divided / In three our kingdom" (I.i. 38–39), reminiscent of the early "knowing" of Othello. What Lear does throughout this scene seems to be done without thought.

---

[12] William Frost has written influentially about the ritualistic beginning of *King Lear* in relation to other plays. See his "Shakespeare's Rituals and the Opening of *King Lear*," *Hudson Review*, X (1958), 577–585. I cannot agree with G. R. Elliott that the mood of the opening passages is almost humorous, that Lear quite rightly prefers Albany to Cornwall, but has in the interest of policy made their shares of the kingdom equal. Since, according to Elliott, Lear is doing an unusual thing in dividing his kingdom, he makes it seem more usual with a public ceremony in which everyone is supposed to play the game. "The Initial Contrast in 'Lear,'" *Journal of English and Germanic Philology*, LVIII (1959), 251–263.

When Goneril and Regan offer their fulsome protestations of love, he makes no comment upon what they have said. When Cordelia gives him logic instead of flattery, he is of course enraged; but he does not really argue or reason with her. Instead, he pronounces his disowning of her: "Let it be so; thy truth, then, be thy dower!" (I.i.110); and the rest of the speech is a ceremonial denunciation that is as final, and as thoughtless, as ritual can make it.

In this ritualistic manner one notes too a turning away from direct address. Instead of "thou," Cordelia becomes "she." This may be partly because she is no longer his child. But the manner is more pervasive than this, extending also to other characters, notably in his curse upon Goneril. Wolfgang Clemen has observed that Lear does not engage in real dialogue.[13] He does not really talk with, let alone argue with, other persons. He will recognize, but not answer objections. To the reasonable protests of Kent, Cordelia, and France, he is as little responsive as though no thought were going on in his mind at all. He might as well be living in a solipsistic world. And yet there are, as there are with Hamlet, no soliloquies at this point. Instead, there are pronouncements, curses, oaths, seldom directed at other characters, though involving them indirectly. This tendency will continue throughout a good part of the play, and is the most serious symptom of a failure to communicate with people or with events—a failure in communication that can at best augur only the kind of insight a Timon of Athens will achieve.

But as the perfidy of Goneril is driven home to him, this kind of apparent thoughtlessness takes a different and more hopeful form. We get clues to the fact that Lear has been thinking, or at least brooding. The first unmistakable sign of reflection appears when a knight tells him that he suspects "a great abatement of kindness" from Goneril. Lear replies:

Thou but rememb'rest me of mine own conception. I have perceived a most faint neglect of late, which I have rather blamed as

[13] *The Development of Shakespeare's Imagery* (New York: Hill and Wang, n.d.), p. 134.

mind own jealous curiosity than as a very pretence and purpose of unkindness. I will look further into't.

(I.iv.72–76)

And when the knight tells him that the Fool has much pined away since Cordelia left for France, Lear replies: "No more of that; I have noted it well" (I.iv.81). Both instances are clues to thought that has taken place privately. At this point in the play Lear has begun to think, and to think in a responsive way. But what is dramatically remarkable and almost new about it is that it has not been put into words. In one respect, then, Lear is the ultimately pensive hero, since he does not even feel the need to communicate his thought. But more important, and more certain, is the obligation put upon the actor to convey Lear's thinking without words.

An extension of this striking way of depicting thought appears in Lear's conversations with the Fool. We shall see in chapter v that the Fool is influential in Lear's self-discovery. But here it is relevant to ask whether Lear really converses with the Fool. They engage in riddles, propounded by the Fool, and there seems to be occasional contact of their minds in banter. But the contact is superficial only. What Lear is seriously thinking about during the banter and the Fool's songs is often unrelated to the conversation. It runs much deeper. When Lear comes forth with a new insight or reflection, it comes seemingly unprepared for, or is more often a delayed reaction to a much earlier provocation. Totally out of the context of immediate conversation are "A pestilent gall to me!" (I.iv.127) and "I did her wrong" (I.v.25). The second of these is so independent of its context that we cannot with certainty say to whom Lear is referring by "her." The usual guess is Cordelia, for this has the advantage of marking an early recognition of the grave mistake he made in the first scene. But D. G. James argues that the "her" is Goneril, for Lear is seeking patience.[14] Moreover, he has been talking to Goneril more recently and he may be trying to salvage his earlier good opinion of her and the rightness of his judgment in trusting in her. In either case, he has been thinking about a larger

---

[14] *The Dream of Learning: An Essay on the Advancement of Learning, Hamlet, and King Lear* (Oxford: Clarendon Press, 1951), p. 95.

moral issue (and about himself) even while he has been giving practical directions ("Go you before to Gloucester with these letters".) and jesting with the Fool.

One of the most dramatically successful results of this kind of interrupted, scattered, or subterranean thought is that it is an improvement on the soliloquy. In *King Lear* Shakespeare might seem to have lost the faculty or inducement for the use of soliloquy, perhaps because he no longer has the proper kind of meditative hero. But Lear does, as we have intimated, become a meditative hero. He does not simply turn to the audience and give a coherent account of what he is thinking. In *King Lear* the soliloquy is for the most part relegated to an inferior character, Edmund, and it is shown to be far less effective for the representation of live thought than the interrupted kind of meditation. The best example of what might have been a soliloquy is a series of thoughts dispersed throughout a long dialogue in the passage beginning Act I, scene v, already alluded to in part. Out of a passage of fifty-one lines, there are only a scattered few that mark the progress of Lear's meditation. Put together they would form this soliloquy: "I did her wrong— . . . I will forget my nature. So kind a father! . . . O, let me not be mad, not mad, sweet heaven! / Keep me in temper; I would not be mad!" Such a dispersal of thought is an improvement, at least for stage presentation, upon even the highly dramatic incoherence of Hamlet's "O, what a rogue and peasant slave am I," or upon the more obvious kind of incoherence that precedes Othello's falling into a fit.

Still another aspect of Lear's personality which is apparently most unpromising for the development of thought is his habit of commanding. This, too, is related to his inability to engage in dialogue. The earliest commands are of course totally unpropitious for insight. They are the disowning of Cordelia and the banishment of Kent. There is no flexibility to them, no tempering of harsh imperiousness with reflection upon what he is doing. One would expect the storm, that great agent and symbol of affliction, to alter this habit of mind. At first it does not do so. In Act III, Lear

> Bids the wind blow the earth into the sea,
> Or swell the curled waters 'bove the main,
> That things might change or cease. . . .
>
> (III.i.5-7)

Gradually there enters a small degree of thoughtful purpose into what he demands of the elements. The thunder is to

> Strike flat the thick rotundity o' th' world!
> Crack nature's moulds, all germens spill at once
> That makes ingrateful man!
>
> (III.ii.7-9)

But still, despite Lear's growing interest in generation and his conviction that creation is corrupt, this demand is mainly an enlargement from microcosm to macrocosm of his private tantrums. So too is the next outburst ("Rumble thy bellyful! Spit, fire! Spout, rain!"). The substance of these commands is, however, a turning from rage to a pitying awareness of old age; but of course the old age is limited to his own personal situation.

Thenceforth, however, the great commands begin to carry much of the burden of thought in the play. Lear cannot learn by arguing, with others or with himself. He has only one way of sustained meditation, and this is by command. It is by a series of commands that he first reaches his perceptions into social corruption and injustice:

> Tremble, thou wretch
> That hast within thee undivulged crimes,
> Unwhipp'd of justice! Hide thee, thou bloody hand;
> Thou perjur'd, and thou simular of virtue
> That art incestuous! Caitiff, to pieces shake,
> That under covert and convenient seeming
> Has practis'd on man's life! Close pent-up guilts,
> Rive your concealing continents, and cry
> These dreadful summoners grace.[15]
>
> (III.ii.51-59)

---

[15] See also the later command, "Thou rascal beadle, hold thy bloody hand!" (IV.vi.164).

Notice that these speeches, too, have some of the function of soliloquy. They are addressed, to be sure, to the elements or to persons imagined as present, but essentially they show Lear in private thought.

The curses, too, have something of this progression. They move from the rigid disowning of Cordelia to the curse on Goneril (I.iv.297–311). This curse is mainly one of angry, frustrated self-pity, but we shall see in the last chapter that it represents the beginning of Lear's interest in the sexuality of women.

There is also a progression, of a sort, in Lear's ability to argue. True, he argues very little, and only once or twice with himself. But when we remember that at first he merely commands and curses and never crosses minds with another character, any change is for the better. His most characteristic form of argument is not particularly subtle. We see it best in his dispute with Kent over who has put the Earl in the stocks:

> *Kent.*   *It is both he and she;*
> *Your son and daughter.*
> *Lear. No.*
> *Kent. Yes.*
> *Lear. No, I say.*
> *Kent. I say, yea.*
> *Lear. No, no; they would not.*
> *Kent. Yes, they have.*
> *Lear. By Jupiter, I swear, no.*
>
> (*II.iv.13–20*)

Although this scarcely sparkles as repartee, Lear is beginning to feel the necessity of dialogue.

Earlier, he had been compelled to argue with Goneril about his "insolent retinue." Upon hearing Goneril's incredible rebuke of his knights and the implied censure of himself, he does not at first even try to argue with her. He asks, instead, with incredulity, "Are you our daughter?" (I.iv.238), and "Your name, fair gentlewoman?" (I.iv.257). There is something pathetically like an ancient clown in the behavior that Goneril coldly calls Lear's "pranks"; and Regan later (II.iv) calls them "unsightly tricks" when Lear, upon hearing that he must return to Goneril and ask her forgiveness, grotesquely (in a manner recalling Richard II's theatrics) falls to his knees.

> *Ask her forgiveness?*
> *Do you but mark how this becomes the house:*
> *"Dear daughter, I confess that I am old;*
> *Age is unnecessary. On my knees I beg*
> *That you'll vouchsafe me raiment, bed, and food."*
>
> *(II.iv.154–158)*

Lear has probably never before in his life had to argue. Placed in this preposterous situation, he cannot react with any reasoned remonstrance. Never having learned to think, and now placed in a situation of stress, he can only ludicrously dramatize his sense of outrage and self-pity.

His inability to argue with his daughters is shown most effectively when he confronts the two of them at Gloucester's castle. To Regan's request that he return to Goneril, he replies with a passionate speech expressing almost tearfully what he would rather do than return. Her cold, terse response is devastatingly adequate: "At your choice, sir" (II.iv.220), and Lear can only, in protest, cry out, "I prithee, daughter, do not make me mad" (II.iv.221). When Regan continues to refuse and rebuke him, pointedly referring to her ability to "mingle reason with your passion" (II.iv. 237), he responds weakly: "Is this well spoken?" (II.iv.239). And when she does make an apparent concession, but with the cruel, unacceptable condition that he keep only twenty-five knights, he says, with total helplessness, "I gave you all" (II.iv.253).

What is therefore surprising is that when they have reduced him by their reasoning to no followers at all ("What need one?"), he begins to argue in a way far more profound than his daughters, with their merely wily intelligence, are capable of.[16] I refer, of course, to his powerfully emotional but also philosophical "O, reason not the need!" (II.iv.267).

---

[16] For the kind of "reason" in Goneril and Regan, see Terence Hawkes, *Shakespeare and the Reason: A Study of the Tragedies and the Problem Plays* (London: Routledge & Kegan Paul, 1964), chap. vi.

In the final chapter we shall see how this speech contributes to his self-discovery. Here may be noted only—besides its sudden advance from no argument, to weak argument, to profound argument—that it exemplifies one of the most dramatic methods Shakespeare ever devised for the depiction of man thinking. It is not an impressively coherent argument. The disquisition on "true need" occupies only seven lines and is never completed because Lear is suddenly overcome by self-pity.

What is dramatically, and intellectually, imposing about the speech is what it reveals about the growing flexibility of Lear's mind. His thought changes direction several times during the speech. Much of this, to be sure, is the result of sheer frustration and passion. But there is also shown an ability to shift position, to change the direction of thought in midcareer. A better example of this kind of sudden change in the direction of thought—here clearly marking a new insight even as he is speaking—occurs when Lear is told that Cornwall will not see him. His first response is his earlier kind of unreflective fury:

> *The King would speak with Cornwall; the dear father*
> *Would with his daughter speak, commands her service.*
> *Are they "inform'd" of this? My breath and blood!*
> *"Fiery"? The fiery duke? Tell the hot duke that—*

And then comes one of the first moments of self-doubt Lear has had. He proceeds:

> *No, but not yet; may be he is not well.*
> *Infirmity doth still neglect all office*
> *Whereto our health is bound; we are not ourselves*
> *When nature, being oppress'd, commands the mind*
> *To suffer with the body. I'll forbear;*
> *And am fallen out with my more headier will,*
> *To take the indispos'd and sickly fit*
> *For the sound man.—*

But then, upon his recalling that Kent is in the stocks, comes still another change in direction:

> *Death on my state! Wherefore*
> *Should he sit here? This act persuades me*
> *That this remotion of the Duke and her*
> *Is practice only.*
>
> (*II.iv.102–116*)

This is more than incoherent thought; it is a progression of thought as new evidence comes to his mind.

In contrast with the earlier meditative heroes, there is little sense of costume in Lear as thinker. Shakespeare seems to want to show that here is the real thing: man unselfconsciously learning to think. The closest that Lear comes to posture in thought is when he beats his head in exasperation at his folly (I.iv.292–294). There is likewise a faint hint of stage effect when later, in madness, Lear goes through some of the motions of being a serious student. He wants to be associated with Poor Tom, the "philosopher":

> *I'll talk a word with this same learned Theban.*
> *What is your study?*
>
> (*III.iv.162–163*)

Perhaps the *your* should be stressed, indicating that Lear is a fellow scholar with his own specialty, which happens to be unkind daughters.

In place of the old-fashioned techniques of showing a hero intent upon thought, Shakespeare substitutes for Lear the hero's terrible struggle to remain sane, to remain in a condition that permits him to think and learn. Lear's first intimations of insanity perhaps disturb him mainly by the panic they cause—a panic in part due to the premonition that he will, if insane, lose the commanding role in life which is part of his very identity. If insane, he will no longer be in control of himself or others. But he at any rate struggles— apparently the first struggle with his own mind in the play:

> *O, let me not be mad, not mad, sweet heaven!*
> *Keep me in temper; I would not be mad!*
>
> (*I.v.50–51*)

Later, he resolutely tries to keep from thinking on his fixation, his unkind daughters, for "that way madness lies; let me shun that" (III.iv.21).

We see later that he really wishes to maintain his power of thought. The "tempest in my mind" is terrible and at first prevents him from feeling the impact of the storm:

> When the mind's free,
> The body's delicate; the tempest in my mind
> Doth from my senses take all feeling else
> Save what beats there.
>
> (*III.iv.11–14*)

But he revises this opinion and declares the storm an anesthesia to the more painful thoughts. He at first refuses to go into the shelter:

> Prithee, go in thyself; seek thine own ease.
> This tempest will not give me leave to ponder
> On things would hurt me more.
>
> (*III.iv.23–25*)

Then, in one of his most important decisions—one that should be stressed in acting—he resolves: "But I'll go in." Going in leads both to new insight and, in the almost unbearable struggle of thought, to madness.

What he most fears, madness, does come upon him in this scene (III.iv), once he has insulated himself from what is usually referred to—not quite accurately, I think—as the purgatorial storm. It is the effects of the storm that, to be sure, serve to illustrate for him some basic truths about himself and man. But the storm itself is a protection against "things would hurt me more."

A more difficult question is whether Lear's madness similarly serves to insulate him from these more painful things.[17] Glouces-

---

[17] Critical views on the "reason" in Lear's madness differ, but three major critics agree that it does not detract from his insights. Robert B. Heilman writes: "Lear, who in the normal state is . . . weak on implication and synthesis, shows, amid the irrelevancies of madness, an organizing imagination of considerable power and actually puts together a coherent general view of

ter, with his superficial view of life, believes that it does. He wishes, in his affliction, that he could have the King's anesthesia of madness:

> *Better I were distract;*
> *So should my thoughts be sever'd from my griefs,*
> *And woes by wrong imaginations lose*
> *The knowledge of themselves.*
>
> (*IV.vi.288–291*)

Even today this is the popular view of madness: that its unreal, occasionally grotesque kind of thinking is an escape from painful thought. Actually, modern psychology knows that, though they may be fantastically mistaken, thoughts of the most painful intensity go on beneath the seemingly irresponsible surface of madness. When he came to write *King Lear*, Shakespeare had already had occasion, in *Hamlet*, to show not only that madness is a kind of thinking; it often is a thinking closer to one's deepest nature than the controlled thinking of sanity. In an Ophelia, of course, the result of madness is mainly grotesque exhibitionism. Yet there is something in her antics which is significant enough to disturb her friends. She

> *speaks things in doubt*
> *That carry but half sense. Her speech is nothing,*
> *Yet the unshaped use of it doth move*

experience, a symbolic formulation of the problem of evil as set forth in the world of the play; the mental failure caused by the pressure of circumstances is not only a failure but an escape, a means of liberating for full flight an imagination that was hampered before." *This Great Stage: Image and Structure in King Lear* (Seattle: University of Washington Press, 1963; originally published 1948), p. 181. According to A. C. Bradley, Lear's madness stimulates "that power of moral perception and reflection which had already been quickened by his sufferings." *Shakespearean Tragedy* (New York: Meridian Books, Inc., 1960; first published 1904), p. 231. Wolfgang Clemen states (*The Development of Shakespeare's Imagery*, p. 151): "Lear's insanity should not be dismissed as simple craziness. It is rather another manner of perception, by means of which Lear now sees and recognizes what formerly remained concealed to him, as long as he was sane." An important article on Lear's insights during his insanity is Kenneth Muir's "Madness in *King Lear*," *Shakespeare Survey* 13 (1960), pp. 30–40.

> The hearers to collection. They aim at it
> And botch the words up fit to their own thoughts;
> Which, as her winks and nods and gestures yield them,
> Indeed would make one think there would be thought,
> Though nothing sure, yet much unhappily.
>
> (*IV.v.6–13*)

There is no method in poor Ophelia's madness. Unlike Hamlet's antic disposition, it can conceal nothing. She says things that are so shocking that for a century the deeply self-revealing parts of her mad scenes were cut in performance. The trouble with this for our purposes, however, is that although we gain a better knowledge of Ophelia through these scenes, the unhappy girl herself does not. On the other hand, Hamlet's more controlled madness, if it is really that, permits his intelligence to work with feverous, if not always accurate, effect. And even if Hamlet is not mad, what Polonius says about his antic behavior is probably a clue to the way the audience would understand perceptive distraction of this sort:

> How pregnant sometimes his replies are! a happiness that often madness hits on, which reason and sanity could not so prosperously be deliver'd of.
>
> (*II.ii.212–214*)

Lear's thought in madness seems to lie somewhere midway between Ophelia's and Hamlet's. It is obviously less controlled than Hamlet's, and yet it has (along with many irrational insights) an awareness, a responsibleness far more significant for self-discovery than the totally profitless self-exhibitionism of Ophelia. Lear is assuredly the best example of madman as thinker in all literature.

But his madness is not at first conducive to advancement in learning. Indeed, the first indication that he is aberrant in thought shows a fixation, a conviction that all his and the world's troubles are caused by unkind daughters. His first really irrational utterance occurs at III.iv.65,[18] when, upon seeing Edgar acting as a madman, he diagnoses the case as the result of ungrateful daughters:

[18] I disagree with Sholom J. Kahn in his assertion that Lear does not go mad until Act IV. " 'Enter Lear mad,' " *Shakespeare Quarterly*, VIII (1957), 311–329.

> *Has his daughters brought him to this pass?*
> *Couldst thou save nothing? Wouldst thou give 'em all?*

This might appear to be merely another of Lear's "pranks," the kind of self-dramatizing that he has no mean skill in. But when Kent tells him that Poor Tom has no daughters, Lear's violent reaction shows the terrible rigidity of his fixation:

> *Death, traitor, nothing could have subdu'd nature*
> *To such a lowness but his unkind daughters.*
>
> (*III.iv.72–73*)

This fixation stubbornly recurs; and the removal of it—never perhaps total and noticeable only after his recovery—is one of his steps toward insight. But even while he is still fully under the delusion, he begins, in madness, to probe with increasing inquisitiveness into the nature of man and the world. For instance, while still regarding his daughters as the cause of all corruption, he begins to do more than curse them; he would, now that he "will keep still with my philosopher" (III.iv.181), approach the problem as a student. He stages the bizarre "trial" of Goneril and Regan as an attempt to deal rationally with these creatures. Then he would, as a student of anatomy, examine Regan:

Then let them anatomize Regan; see what breeds about her heart. Is there any cause in nature that make these hard hearts?

> (*III.vi.80–82*)

The important word is *cause*. He is beginning to inquire, as Renaissance texts recommend, into the anatomy to see why man is what he is. And one of the first questions he asks of Poor Tom, "this philosopher," is "What is the *cause* of thunder?" (III.iv. 160). Earlier he had merely commanded the elements, "the thunder would not peace at my bidding" (IV.vi.103–104), but now he wants to discover why.

These, however, are merely foreglimpses of the greater insights he will achieve and of the new flexibility and inquisitiveness of his mind in madness. In later chapters we shall see some of the spe-

cific questions he asks of himself and others. These are of course
far from being entirely the result of madness. Much of his self-
inquiry occurs when he is sane, or nearly so; much of its most
accurate activity comes when he awakens exhausted and recovered.
But what I would stress here, since the concern of this chapter has
been the thinking process in general, is that probably without the
madness—a madness always alternating with and sharpening
lucidity—Lear would not have uncovered so many truths about
himself as he does. It is probably no accident that the hero who
learns most about himself is forced beyond the threshold of madness to do so. And it is no accident that the drama of self-discovery
is made far more intense, more painful, and more exhausting by
the hero's madness. For even we that are young see the whole
journey through Lear's aged and bewildered eyes.

IV
Other Characters
on the Rack
of This Tough World

It is not simply the agony of the learning process which forces Lear over the brink of madness. It is also "the rack of this tough world" in which he lives as an old, rejected man. This world, in its "thick rotundity," is probably the most "tough," the most adamant one in Shakespearean drama, and it is Lear rather than the world who will have to change. It is a world of intransigent nature, both human and nonhuman. The nonhuman one will not yield to his commands: it will not alter its severity; things will not "change or cease" (III.i.7) despite the crying need of his pathetically feeble condition. "For the rain it raineth every day." [1]

But at least this nonhuman one is not an "unkind" world. It is the obduracy of the human world which proves the greater torment to the King. This is made up of Cordelia with her "nothing"; of the totally inflexible evil daughters; of the brutal Cornwall, whose indoor form of cruelty adds the exquisitely "human" touch to the indiscriminate fury of the elements; of Kent with whom argument is impossible ("I say, yea"); and of the Fool who, despite his lack of controlled intelligence, is as "bitter" and relentless as the elements in the unarguable rigor of his tutelage.

But these, and other characters, are more than cruelly unchanging forces to an old man in desperate need of solicitous adaptability. They are foils to Lear in a drama of self-discovery. They

[1] See James Land Jones, *"King Lear* and the Metaphysics of Thunder," *Xavier University Studies,* III (1964), 51–80, and Max Lüthi, "Themen und Motive im Werk Shakespeares," *Schweizer Monatshefte,* XLIV (1964), 59–70, both of which have interesting things to say about the *King Lear* world, particularly the presence or absence of a moral order and (notably Lüthi's article) the monstrous aspects of life counterbalanced by quiet effects.

embody, along with the less adamant Edmund, Edgar, and Gloucester, varying degrees of simplicity, adamancy, and unchangeability; and against this background, some of which pointedly parallels Lear's own, the miracle of an even more adamant old man changing is much the greater.

The simplest of the characters is Kent. Much could, with ingenuity, be made of Kent's character and his need for some kind of recognition. There is something touching in the last scene, when, trying so hard to be recognized by his delirious master, he finds that only a small part of his role in Lear's pilgrimage can be communicated. But he is more dramatically significant if regarded not as one of several characters uneasy as to who he is, or being forced to adapt to an unchanging world, but rather, in his self-sufficiency, as an absolute foil to Lear. He knows who he is. He thinks that he knows perfectly well who Lear is: his master, one whom he has loved as his father, and one who has authority. When in disguise he is asked by Lear who he is, he replies, "A man, sir" (I.iv.11); and he is really not very different in disguise from what he is in his true status. His blunt answer may seem pointless, or merely a part of his rough pose. But learning to answer the same question in much the same way will be one of Lear's most meaningful achievements. This is not of course to say that Lear in self-discovery will attain only the uncomplicated mind of a Kent; but Kent in his simplicity represents one facet of the total complex of man that Lear will have to learn himself to be. What, however, is most important about Kent for our present purposes is that he doesn't change, doesn't learn. His uncomplicated view of life does not seem to have been altered, though it has been challenged, by all the ordeals he has gone through with his master. He stands up, without asking any questions at all, against the most unyielding forces of nature and man. Perhaps his most revealing remark occurs when he is put in the stocks: "Sir, I am too old to learn." We discover elsewhere that he is forty-eight; Lear is eighty.

For the wicked characters, with the exception of Edmund, there is no hint of change or self-discovery. Perhaps better than mere simplicity, the two evil daughters represent the adamant quality of the *King Lear* world. Their minds are supple enough merely to outwit a foolish old man and to shift their outward natures as expediency demands, but not to inquire into themselves. When the world challenges them in the form of a storm, they go indoors. They are capable of a modicum of analytical thought when they diagnose their father's foolishness as that of an old man who has always but slenderly known himself, but this is simply an easy way of shifting the illumination from themselves. They are not generally good judges of character. Goneril is totally and disastrously wrong when she ascribes her husband's virtue to an unmanly nature. And both prove easy dupes for Edmund. They have absolutely no inclination toward learning anything, particularly if learning will prove painful. Their attitude toward learning is best summed up in Goneril's advice to her husband: "Never afflict yourself to know more of it" (I.iv.313). And when Albany advises Goneril, "See thyself, devil!" (IV.ii.59), she replies only, "O vain fool!"

Cordelia represents a different form of adamancy. She, like her sisters, serves to show how stubbornness and inflexibility run in the entire Lear family. Possibly she does regret the results of her early rigor, though to the very end, so far as I can discover, she puts the blame entirely on her sisters and not once on herself. At any rate, her function in the drama, particularly if it is a symbolic one, is far too enigmatic to permit adequate treatment here. It will suffice to emphasize that she, like most of the other characters, represents adamancy in thought, and that whatever change of mind she may undergo is characterized more by pity and love, always latent within her, than by painful recognition.[2] Perhaps, like Isabella in *Measure for Measure*, she does learn that she must make some compromise with the human condition and with a tough world; but the learning is never expressed. She does, however, share with Edgar and Lear one ability—perhaps the most meaningful one in a

[2] Harley Granville-Barker finds Cordelia to be an unchanging, simple character: "Cordelia is never in doubt about herself. . . . There is not, at any time, much to explain in Cordelia. Nor does she now herself protest her love and express her forgiveness. She has not changed; elaboration would only falsify her." *Prefaces to Shakespeare*, First Series (London: Sidgwick & Jackson, Ltd., 1949), pp. 190–191.

play where humanity tries to assert itself against an unfeeling world—the ability to weep.

Edmund is a still more interesting kind of simplicity and adamancy. Even more than with Kent, a good case could be made for his humanity. He suffers from the good-natured, but nevertheless humiliating attitude of his father toward him as a bastard. He is obviously deeply motivated to prove his worth. Indeed, as a bastard, he would have more motive than anyone else in the play to establish—though not necessarily to discover—his own identity. Probably his most significant line in the play, suggesting his genuine need for recognition, is "Yet Edmund was belov'd!" (V.iii. 239). There are all the materials here for a complex characterization. It is as though Shakespeare had recalled his forfeited opportunity in *Richard III* and was once more on the brink of giving a worthy role to an unloved, but talented and ambitious, man. But once again, I feel, he did not choose to do so. It was more important that Edmund, in his total honesty about himself and in the clarity and unchanging nature of his insight, serve as a foil to Lear.

It is he, rather than Lear, who has the soliloquies of self-inspection; but they come at the beginning of the play. He knows himself once and for all, and without any illusions or sentimentality, upon his first appearances. But what he knows about himself is limited by what he is and by his habit of controlling rather than studying experience. Nature, and nature in the stark sense that Lear finds an enemy to his humanity, is his goddess. It is unlikely that with more affliction he would have been a more profound character. Total cynicism has been his only tactic for living with himself in an unkind world; and cynicism, as the careers of Richard III and Iago testify, can be a blind alley to understanding.

Along with Albany (who is not significantly characterized), Edgar represents that quality of humanity which tries to assert its more human features in a tough world. Edgar is unquestionably an adaptable personality, the most adaptable in the play. But so changing is his role, and so tied is it to the function of plot and the development of two major characters, that it has been argued, notably by Leo Kirschbaum, that he is no character at all. Linking his role with that of Banquo in *Macbeth*, Kirschbaum writes:

Edgar is not a mimetic unity; he is a dramatic device. Each of his roles contributes not to a rich psychological unity but to Shakespeare's poetic purposes. True, Edgar has a basic plot function, that of being the dispossessed son. But his various roles do not tell us more about Edgar. They tell us more about the play in which he is a character.[3]

This assessment does not, however, take adequately into account Shakespeare's almost unique ability, even while making full use of function, to transform function into character.

But Kirschbaum is obviously in part right. It is precisely because of Edgar's frequent shifts in outward persona that it is difficult to trace a steady growth in his inner point of view. A firm basis is lacking. Like Lear he undergoes a journey of ordeal and enlightenment, but unlike Lear's journey, it has no clear point of origin. We do not know precisely what it is that Edgar is proceeding *from*. His early role in the play is too passive, indeed almost too contemptible, to elicit any interest in what will happen to him. When he first enters, it is to the derisive accompaniment of Edmund's "pat he comes like the catastrophe of the old comedy" (I.ii.146). He has, like Gloucester, the great disadvantage of being first seen through Edmund's comically appraising eyes. In this light he seems to be a rather amiable simpleton:

> a brother noble,
> *Whose nature is so far from doing harms*
> *That he suspects none; on whose foolish honesty*
> *My practices ride easy.*
>
> *(I.ii.195–198)*

But Professor Mack, although not much impressed by Edgar as an individual character, takes good advantage of the Morality tradition to suggest Edgar's kinship with one type of Morality hero, "the naïf and dupe who out of deception and harsh experience gains wisdom." [4] Though starting in the capacity of an inno-

---

[3] *Character and Characterization in Shakespeare* (Detroit: Wayne State University Press, 1962), p. 61.

[4] Maynard Mack, *King Lear in Our Time* (Berkeley and Los Angeles: University of California Press, 1965), p. 62.

cent—a noble one, we should insist—Edgar does more than serve an illustrative or tutoring function for other characters; he makes a development in his own right, and in a world that demands radical education of its more human inhabitants, those who do not choose, like Cornwall, Goneril, and Regan, to go indoors.

Once Edgar has, as had Lear and Gloucester in a less real sense, been dispossessed and exiled, he starts like the others upon what he later calls his "pilgrimage" (V.iii.196). He does so, far more than Lear or Gloucester, as a "nothing" without a figure. He represents the tabula rasa of the play, the man who must start entirely without accommodation. In his very "nakedness," he says, he will confront the tough world, "The winds and persecutions of the sky" (II.iii.11–12). It will be observed that the need for disguise in itself did not necessitate this kind of disguise. He apparently, in a lesser way than Lear, wants to find out what humanity means in a tough world. He has in addition lost even his own identity, more completely than Lear or Gloucester: "Edgar I nothing am" (II.iii. 21). At the end of the play he reiterates this important loss: "Know, my name is lost" (V.iii.121). This is another aspect of his nakedness. No other character in the play faces so immediately and intimately a world seemingly indifferent to him, and even hostile to his being an individual human being.

If Edgar must be taken as a "function" in the play, that function is surely the learning, through total nakedness, what man must learn to endure and *feel* in the mere process of survival. This is a kind of self-discovery. In his career as Poor Tom, he is not merely a wildly chattering antic. He is a *feeling* man. He feels for himself, of course: "Tom's a-cold" (III.iv.59); and in defending himself against the fiends, he is symbolically suffering what his father suffers more clearly, a struggle with the temptation of sacrilegious resentment and despair. But he also suffers for all of humanity. Unlike the Fool, who represents an unchangingly severe view of human folly, Edgar as a human being is repeatedly compelled to step out of his comforting disguise and express one human being's compassion for another. Of the mad King, he says in an aside:

My tears begin to take his part so much,
They mar my counterfeiting.

(*III.vi.63–64*)

He learns the universality of suffering mankind and enlarges his
sympathies by recognizing

How light and portable my pain seems now,
When that which makes me bend makes the King bow.

(*III.vi.115–116*)

He beautifully summarizes what he has learned in his pilgrimage
as "the art of known and *feeling* sorrows." When his father asks
him who he is, he replies:

A most poor man, made tame to fortune's blows;
Who, by the art of known and feeling sorrows,
Am pregnant to good pity.

(*IV.vi.225–227*)

This, though it is not so powerfully prepared for, is even better
than Lear's "I am a very foolish fond old man," and better than
Lear's pity expended mainly on himself:

I should ev'n die with pity,
To see another thus.

(*IV.vii.53–54*)

But both recognitions are important assessments of the pathetic
human condition.

As the naked man in the play, Edgar is the best qualified to assay
the ultimate in human degradation. It is better, he finds, to be the
lowest, even though contemned, if one knows it. He at least owes
nothing to a hard universe:

Welcome, then,
Thou unsubstantial air that I embrace!
The wretch that thou hast blown unto the worst
Owes nothing to thy blasts.

(*IV.i.6–9*)

The grim lesson of man's courage necessary to face up to what must at times seem to him a meaningless pilgrimage is well expressed in Edgar's most famous lines:

> What, in ill thoughts again? Men must endure
> Their going hence even as their coming hither;
> Ripeness is all.
>
> (V.ii.9–11)

This lesson is not far removed from Lear's own perception of what man must accept as the human predicament in a world that he did not choose, which will not yield to his importunities, at birth or at death:

> When we are born, we cry that we are come
> To this great stage of fools.
>
> (IV.vi.186–187)

In a minor, but not insignificant way, then, Edgar's problems parallel Lear's as well as serving as an exemplum for Lear's self-discovery. But the two are meaningfully distinct. Lear's education on the rack of this tough world is a terminal one. He is preparing for the grave. Edgar, as an untried youth, begins from nothing and, with the resilience of youth, is being educated in what Malcolm calls the "king-becoming graces,"

> As justice, verity, temp'rance, stableness,
> Bounty, perseverance, mercy, lowliness,
> Devotion, patience, courage, fortitude. . . .
>
> (Macbeth IV.iii.92–94)

It is, then, Edgar who will be called upon to help "Rule in this realm, and the gor'd state sustain" (V.iii.320).

It is of course Gloucester who serves as the most important foil to Lear, and criticism has universally celebrated Shakespeare's artistry in paralleling the careers of the two old men.[5] Gloucester is not only a smaller model of Lear; he is a contrasting example of

---

[5] The standard criticism on the subject is that by A. C. Bradley, *Shakespearean Tragedy* (New York: Meridian Books, Inc., 1960; first published 1904), p. 235.

response to circumstances and a cruel world that force him to reevaluate himself.

Instead of Lear's imperious and ritualistic kind of inflexibility at the beginning of the play, Gloucester has a moral rigidity and blindness. He has so often had to acknowledge his bastard son that by now he is "braz'd to't" (I.i.11). He is fundamentally a weak, self-indulgent sensualist who has come to terms with himself. This self-reconciliation has meant adopting a comfortable philosophy of fatalism. Unlike both his sons (who have their own ways of responding to the *King Lear* world), he blames the stars for what has happened to the Lear family and to himself. Edmund scornfully exposes the foolish and cowardly self-evasiveness of his father:

This is the excellent foppery of the world, that, when we are sick in fortune,—often the surfeits of our own behaviour,—we make guilty of our disasters the sun, the moon, and stars, as if we were villains on necessity, fools by heavenly compulsion, knaves, thieves, and treachers by spherical predominance, drunkards, liars, and adulterers by an enforc'd obedience of planetary influence, and all that we are evil in, by a divine thrusting on.

(I.ii.128–137)

This, as Edmund concludes, is "an admirable evasion of whoremaster man, to lay his goatish disposition on the charge of a star!" Gloucester's defeatist view of misfortune, combined with a growing sentimentalism and self-pity, proves to be an almost insurmountable barrier to change and insight.

But once Gloucester has been physically blinded, he begins to see:

I stumbled when I saw. Full oft 'tis seen,
Our means secure us, and our mere defects
Prove our commodities.

(IV.i.21–23)

He is no longer morally blind or "braz'd." As with Lear, the anesthesia of his ability to feel is at least temporarily lifted. He makes his one great speech of insight into the essential responsibility of man for his own sins. Giving his purse to his disguised son, he comments:

> That I am wretched
> Makes thee the happier; heavens, deal so still!
> Let the superfluous and lust-dieted man,
> That slaves your ordinance, that will not see
> Because he does not feel, feel your power quickly;
> So distribution should undo excess,
> And each man have enough.

(IV.i.68–74)

But Gloucester lacks the intellectual strength and resilience of Lear. The philosophy of defeatism is still too attractive for him to survive with the new responsibility born of his momentary insight. Unlike Lear, he would still not quarrel with the "great opposeless wills" of the heavens (IV.vi.38); and to avoid doing so, and out of despair, he attempts a step never once contemplated by Lear: suicide. The recognition that comes of feeling may have been, as it is not for Lear and Edgar, too much for him. At any rate, for the rest of the play he is abjectly nursed from despair by his devoted son; but he never securely fights off the wish for oblivion. He would gladly yield his life to Oswald. And when Edgar, after the King's defeat, tries to lead his father away, Gloucester would prefer to "rot even here" (V.ii.8). To Edgar's remonstrance that men must endure the times of their going hence and coming hither, Gloucester's reply is hardly a strong agreement: "And that's true too." This is his last appearance on stage, even as these are his last words. He dies shortly afterward of a broken heart, "too weak the conflict to support" (V.iii.197) between joy and grief of the final recognition—a recognition of event and not of true identity.[6]

Shakespeare paralleled the stories of Lear and Gloucester partly because they had much in common about the unnatural breaking up of families. But equally important, Gloucester served as a nec-

---

[6] Granville-Barker, who calls Gloucester "the play's nearest approach to the average sensual man" (*Prefaces to Shakespeare*, p. 202), remarks that the one thing this kind of man "cannot endure is knowledge of the truth. Rather death or madness than that!" (p. 205).

essary foil to Lear in the pilgrimage, under affliction, to self-discovery. Under circumstances not too different from Lear's, Gloucester did not learn much about himself. He found, after a brief exposure to feeling and self-responsibility, that an old age spent on the rack of feeling is intolerable. And even though he has learned how to see "feelingly," mere feeling of itself will avail little in this kind of world. In his case it leads to despair. By contrast, Lear progresses beyond feeling, without abandoning it, and asks the great question that asserts the need for human recognition and responsibility in this brutal world. We shall examine that question in the next chapter.

V
Who Is It That
Can Tell Me
Who I Am?

No one man in the play, and certainly not Lear by himself, can supply the answer to this great question for the King. It will by no means be a single or a simple answer. But, as I interpret the play, much of what Lear does learn about himself falls into three categories, unified in part by the persistent quest for what today we should call identity. The categories are these: a need for the reassurance of love and the true meaning of love; an attempt to be recognized by others; and a lesson, largely unsought, from his Fool about his most basic nature. These categories apply principally to Lear as an individual. He needs to know who, as one man, he is. In the next chapter we shall see, with more applicability to Renaissance doctrine, Lear expanding his self-knowledge from himself as an individual to include what it means to be a man.

II
WHICH OF YOU SHALL WE SAY DOTH LOVE US MOST?

The opening scene of *King Lear* is one of the most diversely interpreted in all of Shakespeare, even as it is one of the biggest puzzles.[1] Lear's staging of the "love-contest" seems too ridiculous, too transparently wrong, even if Lear were in his dotage. Equally important, it seems inadequately motivated. Lear gives us only an unsatisfactory explanation for demanding the love protestations:

[1] A survey of critical interpretations of this scene is given by G. R. Elliott, "The Initial Contrast in *Lear*," *Journal of English and Germanic Philology*, LVIII (1959), 251–263.

Which of you shall we say doth love us most,
That we our largest bounty may extend
Where nature doth with merit challenge?

(I.i.52–54)

Except to a very credulous, simpleminded person, this would seem to be an unreliable way of determining "where nature doth with merit challenge." Another problem presented by the scene is Lear's furious reaction to Cordelia's moderate and honest answer to the question. Probably no other circumstance in the play disturbs him more.

One can, as William Frost has done, explain at least part of the unreasonableness of the scene by placing it in the tradition of ritual.[2] This is an attractive theory, for it agrees with our reactions to the scene when it is staged. And it also agrees with what we have noticed about the inflexible manner of Lear early in the play. He does not, we recall, respond with argument or apparent thought to what is said.

But we may, I think, find some degree of motive in what Lear is doing, a motive that would help to account for the violence of his reaction when "rejected" by Cordelia. This motive is connected with the thesis of the present chapter: Lear is seeking some reassurance of identity. One should note carefully, however, that at this point he is seeking reassurance only; nothing could be further from his mind than the labyrinthine complexity of self-exploration into which so simple a question will lead him.

But it is not, of course, so simple a question as he thinks. Love involves, as the entire first scene makes clear, a great deal more than Lear expected it would. To find out how and why one is loved is to learn some basic, complicated, and sometimes unpleasant truths about onself. All that Lear has sought is what most old people need: love—the deepest and most certain evidence that they are wanted and needed. No matter how apparently secure a man may be in position, he cannot do without the most basic of

[2] "Shakespeare's Rituals and the Opening of King Lear," Hudson Review, X (1958), 577–585.

emotional needs. Richard II, in a sensitive utterance, describes well what Lear may feel but does not, perhaps out of pride, say:

> Throw away respect,
> Tradition, form, and ceremonious duty;
> For you have but mistook me all this while.
> I live with bread like you, feel want,
> Taste grief, need friends. . . .
>
> (Richard II III.ii.172–176)

It will take Lear some time to realize the full truth of these lines in relation to himself; but the need for such things is there, though he will not acknowledge it.

What Lear hears about himself in the first two arias of the love avowal is, in its extravagance, not too much in terms of what he wishes to know. Because he at this point believes, or wants to believe, all these things about himself, he does not question the motives behind the protestations.

Cordelia's unpleasant answer to the question is so monstrously wrong—if we can place ourselves momentarily within Lear's mind —that it can only be cruelty, if not indeed imagined only. He hears his favorite daughter's gentle voice telling him something about himself which could come only from a stranger. Hence she will ever after be "as a stranger to my heart and me" (I.i.117).

Because of his present hardness of mind, and because Lear cannot see any truth in this view of love, its message is not immediately useful to him, except for its shock value, in reorienting him toward himself. But though he cannot utilize it immediately, it will, like much else in Lear's learning, go underground. What he learns from Cordelia is the nature of his status as a father: that he has begotten, bred, and loved his child; that she will in return obey, love, and honor him; but when she marries, half her love will go to her husband. This, in the King Lear world, is merely a logical part, one of the unyielding facts of life. But human relationships in this world *can* go beyond the hard facts; and true love is the most important of the relationships to do so. Both Lear, because of his concept of love, and to a lesser extent Cordelia, because of her tactless manner of expressing only one aspect of it,[3] are at fault in this scene. Lear's error, however, is our concern.

It is, I believe, because the meaning of true love is so crucial to Lear's learning about himself that Shakespeare devoted to it most of the remainder of the scene.[4] We do the opening part an injustice if we do not regard it in the light of what Shakespeare made so deliberately its continuing pattern. Kent, who has always loved Lear "as my father," reinforces the lesson given by Cordelia: that a father, or beloved sovereign, is not privileged to behave unreasonably; more specifically, he must make more modest demands of this kind of world, take a humbler view of himself—a lesson that will prove basic to his final self-image.

In addition to the Cordelia "rejection," the whole episode of France's wooing of Cordelia, which Lear must now witness, could tell the King much about his own actions. After Burgundy balks at accepting a dowerless bride, France defines what true love means:

> Love's not love
> When it is mingled with regards that stands
> Aloof from th' entire point.
>
> (I.i.241–243)

In accepting Cordelia, France exemplifies a love of what one is rather than what one owns:

> Fairest Cordelia, that art most rich being poor,
> Most choice forsaken, and most lov'd despis'd!
> Thee and thy virtues here I seize upon,
> Be it lawful I take up what's cast away.
> Gods, Gods! 'tis strange that from their cold'st neglect
> My love should kindle to inflam'd respect.
>
> (I.i.253–258)

[3] Ivor Morris believes that Cordelia deliberately insulted her father through an ironic presentation of his own materialistic point of view. "Cordelia and Lear," *Shakespeare Quarterly*, VIII (1957), 141–158.

[4] An interesting interpretation of "love" in this scene, partially linguistic, is given by Terry Hawkes, " 'Love' in *King Lear*," *Review of English Studies*, X (1959), 178–181. See also Sears Jayne, "Charity in *King Lear*," in *Shakespeare 400: Essays by American Scholars on the Anniversary of the Poet's Birth*, ed.

This is the meaning of the scene as a whole, if Lear could only see it. Ironically, of course, he cannot. He cannot foresee the prompt applicability to himself of the challenge he throws to Burgundy with his rejected daughter:

> Sir, there she stands:
> If aught within that little-seeming substance,
> Or all of it, with our displeasure piec'd,
> And nothing more, may fitly like your Grace,
> She's there, and she is yours.
>
> (I.i.200–204)

It will next be Lear himself who, with "that little-seeming substance," will be on the market of appraisal by the world. He will have to learn then, like Everyman, what his essential worth is and who are his abiding friends.

This he will do; it will be part of his education about himself. But he will not quickly change his view about what constitutes love. Even after he has been disabused of his trust in both Goneril and Regan, and is trying to persuade one of them at least to take him with his retinue, he falls back upon his earlier way of calculating love. To Goneril, who momentarily seems to offer the best terms, he says:

> I'll go with thee.
> Thy fifty yet doth double five and twenty,
> And thou art twice her love.
>
> (II.iv.261–263)

Even after his long ordeal, when he awakens from his madness to discover Cordelia, Lear cannot believe that she loves him:

> I know you do not love me; for your sisters
> Have, as I do remember, done me wrong:
> You have some cause, they have not.
>
> (IV.vii.73–75)

by James G. McManaway (New York: Holt, Rinehart and Winston, Inc., 1964), pp. 277–288; also Robert P. Adams, "King Lear's Revenges," *Modern Language Quarterly*, XXI (1960), 223–227, which deals with Lear's insight into the nature of love as opposed to self-love.

It is only when he and Cordelia are being led off to prison that he is finally reassured about her love and its independence of worldly circumstances, of "Who loses and who wins; who's in, who's out" (V.iii.15). It is also significant that he achieves this perfection of love only after he has been able to say to Cordelia:

> You must bear with me.
> Pray you now, forget and forgive; I am old and foolish.
>
> (IV.vii.84–85)

For true understanding of love must mean for him a true understanding of himself. As long as his autocratic ego demands protestation of total devotion and as long as he sees love as bound to worldly possessions (as in the distribution of land), he cannot have Cordelia's kind of love and the reliable assurance about his own worth which it can give him. Tragically, of course, human love cannot withstand the exigencies of a ruthless world. And the last scene of the play will implicitly substitute another question for that of the first. It will no longer be, Who loves me most? but rather, Of what final reassurance is even true love? Or, more urgently: What am I if Cordelia is nothing?

III
DOTH ANY HERE KNOW ME?

In giving up his kingdom, Lear parallels, as we have seen, the plight of Cordelia put dowerless upon the marriage market. What this means for his self-discovery is considerable, for as long as he retains "all the large effects / That troop with majesty" (I.i.133–134), only his honest counselors will tell him who he is. But it should be noticed that in giving up authority and wealth, he is careful to retain for himself "The name, and all th' addition to a king" (I.i.138). Concerning this attribute, he has an anxious need, for it is, as much as "dear father," an important part of his sense of identity. Earlier Shakespeare had depicted the total loss of identity of a king who was deposed. Richard II laments:

> *I have no name, no title;*
> *No, not that name was given me at the font,*
> *But 'tis usurp'd.*
>
> (*Richard II* IV.i.255–257)

Despite his precautions, Lear will learn that just as he loses one kind of love by giving up authority, so he will forfeit more of his name than he could ever foresee. He will learn that many people indeed do not know him. That is to say, they do not know him as he sees himself.

In the painful pilgrimage that follows, Lear may be seen in the tradition of a parable, that of the Abasement of the Proud King. Maynard Mack has persuasively suggested an archetypal basis, rather than simply a historical source, as an important background for *King Lear*. Mack writes:

In one common form of this archetype, the king comes from swimming or his bath to find his clothes and retainers gone. His role has been usurped by an angel sent from heaven to teach him, in the words of the Magnificat, that God humbles the proud and exalts the humble. In his nakedness, he finds that the evidence of his kingliness, indeed his whole identity, is gone. Assertions that he is in fact the king and efforts to regain his throne lead those around him to mock him as a madman.[5]

I have encountered no other kind of background material that so adequately matches the mountingly nightmarish quality of Lear's growing awareness that he is not what he thought he was. The modern equivalent for this archetypal panic may well be *Angst*. And that the experience of Lear is one timelessly rooted in man's sense of displacement, of alienation, may be seen from the authentic dream of a twentieth-century man. It is graphically related as follows, with the assurance that the dreamer was not neurotic:

---

[5] *King Lear in Our Time* (Berkeley and Los Angeles: University of California Press, 1965), pp. 49–50. For a full discussion of the parable see Lillian Hornstein, "*King Robert of Sicily*: Analogues and Origins," PMLA, LXXIX (1964), 13–21.

The automatic elevator stops with a jolt. The doors slide open, but instead of the accustomed exit, the passenger faces only a blank wall. His fingers stab at buttons: nothing happens. Finally, he presses the alarm signal, and a starter's gruff voice inquires from below: "What's the matter?" The passenger explains that he wants to get off on the 25th floor. "There is no 25th floor in this building," comes the voice over the loudspeaker. The passenger explains that, nonsense, he has worked here for years. He gives his name. "Never heard of you," says the loudspeaker. "Easy," the passenger tells himself. "They are just trying to frighten me."

But time passes and nothing changes. In that endless moment, the variously pleading and angry exchanges over the loudspeaker are the passenger's only communication with the outside world. Finally, even that ceases. . . .[6]

Lear's experience has many of the qualities of both the parable recorded by Mack and the nightmare of modern man. In his new exposure to the world, the first person after Cordelia who does not seem to know him is Kent. By Kent, Lear in his folly is, we recall, addressed bluntly as "old man" (I.i.148). The term of address is an accurate augury of the future. Lear is no longer "your majesty." Just how deliberately meaningful Kent's rude term is, we cannot know. But it does seem that the Earl is meant here to be the mouthpiece of the "tough world." A little later in the play, when Kent is disguised as Caius, Lear asks him, "Dost thou know me, fellow?" (I.iv.28). Kent replies with another accurate appraisal: Lear has that in his countenance which he would *fain* call master, a possible hint that Lear at present is not the man he once worshiped. But, still, Kent is a symbol of loyalty, of the old recognitions. Kent's answers to what will be Lear's agonized questions are given with love.

Lear's question to the disguised Kent is probably asked with some complacence. He has, except for the distressing Cordelia episode and Kent's earlier candor, had no intimations that he is not everything that he believed himself to be. But by the fourth scene

⁶ "The Anatomy of *Angst*," *Time*, March 31, 1961, pp. 44–47 ff.

of the play he has begun to perceive "a most faint neglect" (l. 73). And when he confronts Oswald, already neglectful of him, with a question similar to that he had asked Kent, there may be some uneasiness as well as exasperation in his manner. "Who am I, sir?" he demands (I.iv.86). The answer, "My lady's father," gives him his first real view of his new identity. At this stage of disenchantment he meets every new threat to his self-esteem with rage rather than recognition. It will take a series of shocks to make him ask his question of identity with anxious interest.

The Fool is the next of whom he will learn whether anyone now knows him. So important is the Fool's response that we shall have to view it in a separate section. Here need be noted only Lear's surprised, but probably not too uneasy, "Dost thou call me fool, boy?" (I.iv.162); the Fool's answer, "All thy other titles thou hast given away; that thou wast born with"; and the Fool's most profound description of the diminished Lear, ". . . now thou art an 0 without a figure. I am better than thou art now; I am a Fool, thou art nothing" (I.iv.211–213). Without the "figure," a word connoting rank, stature, trappings, Lear is nothing. And it should be noted that a zero is complete absence of identity.

The most shattering of the new reflections Lear will see of himself is that provided by his two unkind daughters. He "gave [them] all," and to him that is still the definition of what makes for love. He will get from them the most cruelly unflattering of mirrors, much worse than that of Kent or the Fool because it is given with absolute lovelessness by those from whom he had expected unreserved devotion. Goneril addresses him in terms that can be suggested only by the Fool's image of Lear's having made his daughters his mothers: "for when thou gav'st them the rod, and puttest down thine own breeches . . ." (I.iv.188–190). Goneril's "the fault / Would not scape censure" (I.iv.228–229) is exquisitely skillful humiliation, as is her reference to his "new pranks" (I.iv.259).

Lear cannot, as we have seen, argue reasonably with his daughters, or with anyone, at this point. Instead, he asks, not without a histrionic manner, "Are you our daughter?" (I.iv.238). But the

question is more than histrionic; it is, in its most anxious form so
far, the question of whether people know who he is. His daughters
seem to mean most to him, here and throughout the play. If they
do not know him for the "So kind a father" that he is, then he is
indeed a stranger to himself.

This is, in fact, the import of his next series of questions about
himself, which he seems to address to the world about him rather
than merely to Goneril:

> Doth any here know me? This is not Lear.
> Doth Lear walk thus? speak thus? Where are his eyes?
> Either his notion weakens, his discernings
> Are lethargied—Ha! waking? 'Tis not so.
> Who is it that can tell me who I am?
>
> (I.iv.246–250)

This, at least for the purpose of the present study, is one of the
real turning points of the play. For the first time Lear is beginning
with real anxiety to ask who he is. It is an especially significant inquiry, for he is also beginning to see himself objectively. There is
profound psychological insight in Shakespeare's depiction of this
perception by having Lear seem to be at a distance from himself.
He views his body and his motions with a mounting panic.
Though he is thereby beginning a typically Renaissance study of
nosce teipsum, the meaning of the episode is timeless. Lear draws
away in disbelief from this strange image of himself. This body,
which he had always thought himself, cannot really be his. No
one recognizes him, and he does not recognize himself.

But of course his daughters, in their coldly limited way, do know
him. And they have something to tell him which, like Cordelia's,
Kent's, and the Fool's instructions, he will have to incorporate, in
part, into his new self-image, once he is capable of doing so. In
Goneril's opinion, Lear must

> put away
> These dispositions which of late transport you
> From what you rightly are.
>
> (I.iv.241–243)

Because her view of people is uniformly biased by selfishness and a cold heart, she does not fully know of Lear "what you rightly are." But she is correctly aware of many of his faults. As he is old, he should be wise. He should keep men about him such "as may besort your age" (I.iv.272). But above all, what he must learn from her is something that she cannot consciously teach him: that she is indeed his daughter, and that the way she sees him now does not make her a "degenerate bastard" but one who is flesh of his flesh. This insight, however, comes later in the play and must be more fully considered in another context. For the present, Lear can only hold desperately to his preferred self-image, cursing Goneril, denying her charges against him, and threatening:

> Thou shalt find
> That I'll resume the shape which thou dost think
> I have cast off for ever.
>
> (*I.iv.330–332*)

Though he will never be able to resume that former "shape," he will still be able to make a fairly confident attempt to do so by turning to his other daughter, "Who, I am sure, is kind and comfortable" (I.iv.328), who, in other words, will "know" him without his cast-off shape.

The meeting with that other daughter, however, is even more of a blow to his need for recognition. Going to meet Regan at Gloucester's castle, he discovers first that the disguised Kent, an image of himself, since he is "Coming from us" (II.iv.27), has been put in the stocks. Lear's mixture of wrath and uneasiness begins again:

> What's he that hath so much thy place mistook
> To set thee here?
>
> (*II.iv.12–13*)

"Thy place" is really Lear himself, and Lear has again been "mistook." This results in further panic: "O, how this mother swells up toward my heart!" (II.iv.56).

Then Regan will not see him. No one at the castle seems to

know him, though the Duke of Cornwall has been "inform'd."
Lear tries to make himself recognized by shouting his identity:

> The King would speak with Cornwall; the dear father
> Would with his daughter speak, commands her service.
>
> (II.iv.102–103)

Really it is his twin identity he is proclaiming: that of king and of
"dear father." It is to these two notions of himself that he most
desperately clings.

Finally Regan appears, and he greets her with a touchingly anxious need for recognition:

> Beloved Regan,
> Thy sister's naught. O Regan, she hath tied
> Sharp-tooth'd unkindness, like a vulture, here.
> I can scarce speak to thee; thou'lt not believe
> With how deprav'd a quality—O Regan!
>
> (II.iv.135–139)

Here is his last hope of being known (and loved) as he really is.
But once again it is as though "This is not Lear." He hears, instead of the protestations of love he had received from her in their
last meeting, cold words to the effect that the fault is perhaps his
rather than Goneril's. He should, he is once more told, understand
that he is old and unable to judge correctly.

But we should not infer from the daughters' criticisms that they
are interested in rehabilitating the old man through his gaining a
better self-knowledge. Regan's words are the most significant: "I
pray you, father, being weak, seem so" (II.iv.204). What the
daughters want Lear to become in his senility is a mild, incon-
spicuous little man, content with a few old retainers. This is the
kind of old age they had groomed him for:

> They flatter'd me like a dog, and told me I had the white hairs in
> my beard ere the black ones were there.
>
> (IV.vi.97–99)

With a satisfying irony, the daughters prove to be as mistaken
about their father as he had been about them. By "slenderly

known himself," they have meant partly his failure to behave like
a docile old man, attended by a few other docile old men, such as
befit his age. Instead, Lear turns out to be an annoyingly assertive
senior citizen. Rather than accept the reduced role in life they had
planned for him, he resists this diminution, this senility with dynamic wrath. He is no Gloucester being meekly led by the hand
through his bad moments. Rather than submit to the humiliating
kind of recognition his daughters will give him, he will war against
the universe itself.

> No, rather I abjure all roofs, and choose
> To wage against the enmity o' th' air;
> To be a comrade with the wolf and owl,—
> Necessity's sharp pinch.
>
> (II.iv.211–214)

This is, in fact, what he next tries to do. He confronts the ele-
mental forces of nature in his next assayal of whether anyone
knows him. In *As You Like It* Shakespeare had written briefly
about the totally impartial kind of tutelage the elements of nature
will give a man in self-knowledge, equivalent perhaps to the machine today. Contrasting life in the woods with life in the court,
Duke Senior says:

> Here feel we not the penalty of Adam,
> The seasons' difference, as the icy fang
> And churlish chiding of the winter's wind,
> Which, when it bites and blows upon my body
> Even till I shrink with cold, I smile and say,
> "This is no flattery: these are counsellors
> That feelingly persuade me what I am."
>
> (II.i.5–11)

Brutal nature will indeed give Lear a feeling sense of what he is;
but it will not know him—at least as king and as dear father. A
Gentleman describes Lear "contending with the fretful elements,"
commanding them as king. He

> Bids the wind blow the earth into the sea,
> Or swell the curled waters 'bove the main,

That things might change or cease; tears his white hair,
Which the impetuous blasts with eyeless rage
Catch in their fury, and make nothing of. . . .

(III.i.5-9)

"Make nothing of" is significant; the elements do not know even the pathetic quality symbolized by his "white hair." Lear later acknowledges that "the thunder would not peace at my bidding" (IV.vi.103-104), and this is an important lesson learned about what his supposed identity as king means in the storm. But it is not learned without highly dramatic resistance as Lear pleads with the elements to know him. He does not berate their ignorance of him as that of unkind daughters to whom he had given all and who owe him "subscription." Rather:

Here I stand your slave,
A poor, infirm, weak, and despis'd old man;
But yet I call you servile ministers,
That will with two pernicious daughters join
Your high-engender'd battles 'gainst a head
So old and white as this. Oh! Oh! 'tis foul!

(III.ii.19-24)

What the elements do not know about him is that now he is a pathetic figure of an old man. Kent had also told him that he was an old man, and like the storm he had not told him that he was a pathetic one. The pathos is Lear's new tactic for evading the real truths about himself. To benefit from nature's ignorance of him, he will have to resist self-pity; and in a dramatic struggle he does so—at least sufficiently so that it does not bar more important insights.

By not knowing him in his own self-image, the storm teaches him many things. Most of all, as we shall later see, it teaches him a Renaissance lesson about himself as unaccommodated man. It makes him question himself in his capacity as king, not only by refusing to heed his commands but also by forcing him to new insights about justice. In Renaissance terms, again, one of the most important things it does for him is to make him aware of sin, a quality in himself never before mentioned:

> *Close pent-up guilts,*
> *Rive your concealing continents, and cry*
> *These dreadful summoners grace. I am a man*
> *More sinn'd against than sinning.*
>
> (*III.ii.57–60*)

True, he is at first thinking of himself more in the capacity of king
as justicer than as a man on trial. But from the reference to "close
pent-up guilts" and from the later explosion from within him of
the foulest thoughts about sex, which make him feel the need to
cleanse his hand, it is possible that it is in part he who is being
alluded to. Certainly the speech does lead him ultimately to himself. The recognition of himself as at least partially a sinner is a
remarkable one for a man who has previously admitted only one
fault in himself: that he had wronged Cordelia.

There are two later episodes in the play where Lear seems to
need further assurance of his identity. Neither is so searching or
clear-cut as the preceding ones, but they deserve mention for they
suggest how urgent is his need to find from others and from circumstances just who he is.

The first of these episodes is that of Lear in almost complete
delirium, when he enters presumably "fantastically dressed with
wild flowers." In his madness he is not so anxious about who he is
as he was when he felt himself on the brink of madness. Yet the
anxiety is there, even beneath some of his seemingly most assured
declarations of his identity. With no apparent context, he suddenly announces: "No, they cannot touch me for coining; I am
the King himself" (IV.vi.83–84). Just what has been going on in
his tormented mind, we cannot be sure. But he may well imagine
himself in a threatened position, in the midst of an accusing group,
perhaps like that in which he officiated in the mad "trial" scene.
The accusers do not know him. He pleads, despite an awareness
that he has done wrong, that aspect of his identity which formerly
always sustained him: he is a king. Then, in one of his great scenes
of merging recognition, he is identified by the blinded Gloucester
as the King. Lear's response is a regression to his old imperious
manner:

Ay, every inch a king!
When I do stare, see how the subject quakes.

(*IV*.vi.109–110)

But there is a change from the earlier manner, for he is no longer commanding his familiar subjects. The defendants are monsters of sexual depravity. He is king in an unfamiliar world. Again, in the same scene, when friends enter from Cordelia to relieve him, he imagines himself a prisoner beset without rescue. "No seconds?" he cries; "All myself?" (*IV*.vi.198). Thus, imagined alone and facing a world that does not know him, he reverts to his one kind of response:

Come, come; I am a king,
My masters, know you that?

(*IV*.vi.203–204)

It is surely significant that three times in this one scene of greatest madness he should proclaim his identity as king. Perhaps, like Lady Macbeth in her mad scene, he is reliving one of his deepest anxieties. His, of course, is not so much an anxiety of guilt as of who he is, of whether anyone knows him. But beneath an insecurity of identity there is often an anxiety of guilt.

The second episode is that of Lear awakening, after the doctor's ministrations, from his delirium. Here it is natural that he should want to know who he is. It is, in fact, the great recognition scene of the play: the reunion of the shamed, humbled Lear and the solicitous, fully loving Cordelia. Earlier he had not been able to face her, because he thought he knew what she would think of him. Kent had reported:

A sovereign shame so elbows him. His own unkindness,
That stripp'd her from his benediction, turn'd her
To foreign casualties, gave her dear rights
To his dog-hearted daughters,—these things sting
His mind so venomously that burning shame
Detains him from Cordelia.

(*IV*.iii.44–49)

When he now sees her, he is once again convinced that he is a captive, and accused, but now in hell past all judgment. He is "bound / Upon a wheel of fire" (IV.vii.46–47). Then, with gradual recognition, he becomes aware of himself, but still mainly as an unbelievable stranger. The distancing from himself, noticed when he was losing his wits, is repeated as he returns to sanity. It is as though he is asking himself if he knows this man:

> I am mightily abus'd. I should ev'n die with pity,
> To see another thus. I know not what to say.
> I will not swear these are my hands. Let's see;
> I feel this pin prick. Would I were assur'd
> Of my condition!
>
> (IV.vii.53–57)

But now he does become assured of his condition, though with a tentativeness as he faces the full truth of who he is: one still not in his perfect mind, old, and a *man*. Significantly, he no longer mentions his being king.

Perhaps, though, the principal feature of this recognition scene for him lies not in whether others know him; it is—and this is a sign of great advance—whether he knows others. If he can now see his real friends for what they are, as did Everyman, he will also know himself. Cordelia's "Sir, do you know me?" (IV.vii.48) is not only one of the most thrilling questions in the play; it is a crucial one in Lear's self-awakening, for, as we have seen, its satisfactory answer means that he knows the meaning of true love—a relationship demanding that he can face himself for what he is because he is accepted for what he is. But though others will attempt to reassure him that he is a most royal king, he never, in his own mind, will be able to restore the figure to the "0."

IV
DOST THOU CALL ME FOOL, BOY?

On his way toward the answer to the question "Who is it that can tell me who I am?" one of the most important answers Lear receives comes from the Fool. The Fool does know him, but not as Lear has previously seen himself. Lear is recognized as a fellow by his Fool, who, like Kent, always speaks the truth, but does so in wildly oblique, sometimes apparently demented ways.[7] But the Fool, as a source of reassurance to Lear about his identity, obviously means very much to the King. Immediately upon his awareness of insecurity, he begins to ask for his Fool. For one thing, the Fool is closely associated in Lear's mind with the lost Cordelia. But if we accept the interpretation of some critics, that the Fool is one aspect of Lear's own nature, the quest for the Fool is really a quest for a part of himself; and the Fool disappears from the play once that part has been found. However this may be—and it has at least the merit of illuminating vestiges of the Morality play in *King Lear*—what the Fool has to tell Lear about himself is, despite its coming from such a wild spokesman, more profound and ultimately persuasive than what he learns from those who speak more directly and with less sense of the irrationality of life— a quality that is, nonetheless, present simply because the irrational is shown to be the rational in a different guise. It is the world and not the Fool that is irrational; the Fool's wisdom is the wisdom of a cruel world.

For Lear's Fool, if we prosaically examine the content of his speeches and songs, has primarily a practical message for Lear. This is the folly of what he has done at the beginning of the play. The Fool's message, and its early recognition in part, are suggested by Lear's use of the word "folly" upon his realization that Goneril will prove ungrateful and cruel (I.iv.293). In other words, Lear's initial folly is that of mistaken judgment, the kind of tactical error deplored in many of the Renaissance treatises on self-knowledge. It is his first real recognition in the play. But it is first pointed out by the Fool and driven home with relentless repetition, even as a comparable tutor, the rain, raineth every day.

The Fool's first comment, made in Lear's presence, is that Kent

---

[7] Thanks to the researches of Enid Welsford, William Empson, and Robert H. Goldsmith, we now know a good deal about the Elizabethan fool. In our philosophical concern with the Fool, we should never forget, as Alfred Harbage reminds us, that the fool was always very much a source of entertainment.

deserves his own coxcomb "For taking one's part that's out of favour" (I.iv.111–112). Then he offers similar counsel to Lear. If, the Fool says, he had given the daughters "all my living, I'd keep my coxcombs myself. There's mine; beg another of thy daughters" (I.iv.120–122). Here is a clear identification of Lear with the Fool, and for having behaved impractically. Indeed, the prudential content of the Fool's philosophy is apparent even in his songs. His first ditty, far from being a piece of madly inspired wisdom, might have come from Polonius:

> "Have more than thou showest,
> Speak less than thou knowest,
> Lend less than thou owest,
> Ride more than thou goest,
> Learn more than thou trowest,
> Set less than thou throwest;
> Leave thy drink and thy whore,
> And keep in-a-door,
> And thou shalt have more
> Than two tens to a score."

(I.iv.131–140)

I should estimate that about two-thirds of the Fool's comments have to do with Lear's folly in giving all to his daughters and the consequences of his doing so. Here are just a few: "Thou hadst little wit in thy bald crown when thou gav'st thy golden one away" (I.iv.177–178). "Prithee, tell him so much the rent of his land comes to" (I.iv.147–148). "Why, to put's head in; not to give it away to his daughters and leave his horns without a case" (I.v.32–34).

These certainly do not bear out the kindly function of the Fool as described by a Gentleman: the Fool remains with Lear laboring "to outjest / His heart-struck injuries" (III.i.16–17). The Fool is a severe tutor, as are all Lear's schoolmasters, including that part of Lear to which the Fool may correspond: his slowly emerging practical intelligence in a brutal world, a world where it is, as the Fool repeatedly insists, better to stay indoors. If the Fool is not telling Lear that he has behaved impractically, he is assuring the King that without his pompous trappings and his moneybags he is a fool, even a nothing. And these repeated taunts, however affectionate may be their motive, do hurt. Lear, cut by their accuracy, exclaims, "A bitter fool!" (I.iv.150).

But these taunts do lead to more than prudential wisdom. If the Fool were no more instructive than this, he would not be so important a part of the play and Lear would not learn to see himself with the humility that represents a large part of his self-discovery. For one thing, it is the Fool who starts Lear thinking on sex, and perhaps triggers the important sexual fantasies. His allusions to codpiece, whore, and aged lecher are some of the first important sexual images in the play. They help lead Lear to the anatomizing of Regan.

More important still—and this part of his self-discovery must like the foregoing be considered more fully in the next chapter— the Fool by both his philosophy and his status teaches his master that Lear is a fool to begin with, that the human condition is mean and humble. There is profound meaning even in his prudential wisdom. It stresses the fact that the most important truths about man are related to survival and do not make him out to be a very sophisticated creature. Like the Fool, the stripped Lear will have to learn the arts of survival by unbeseeming antics before his "betters." In the company of the Fool, Lear will discover how effective a fool of nature is in confronting a storm.

And there is throughout, never to be underestimated though it is not written into the text, the Renaissance and specifically Erasmian awareness that the simple fool was wiser than the supposed wise man, that to learn true wisdom one must learn the simple virtues of life, like staying with one's master even when practical wisdom discourages it, like seeing through flattery, and like preferring the simplest wisdom of the heart to that of the head.[8] This lesson includes learning to question his own wisdom,

[8] For the Erasmian concept of the Fool, see Willard Farnham, "The Medieval Comic Spirit in the English Renaissance," in *Joseph Quincy Adams Memorial Studies*, ed. by James G. McManaway, Giles Dawson, and Edwin E. Willoughby (Washington, D.C.: Folger Shakespeare Library, 1948), pp. 429–437; and Carolyn S. French, "Shakespeare's 'Folly': *King Lear*," *Shakespeare Quarterly*, X (1959), 523–529.

in full humility. There is far more than a recognition of his practical mistakes in Lear's final words of self-recognition: "I am old and foolish" (IV.vii.85). Certainly the Fool's answers to Lear's question of identity are as accurate as those given by other characters in the play. And they share with the message of the brutal elements the grimly irrational quality of life in its lowest common denominator. They are equally comfortless. But they do have the virtue—not shared by the elements—of answering Lear's questions as if coming from a part of himself.

VI
Is Man No More Than This?

The preceding chapter traces a few of the steps in Lear's progress toward answering the question "Who is it that can tell me who I am?" It will have been noticed that, though Lear is learning much in this progress, the advance is not always explicitly or systematically acknowledged by Lear himself. True, he makes a few key statements:

> I am a man
> More sinn'd against than sinning.
>
> (III.ii.59–60)
>
> I am not ague-proof.
>
> (IV.vi.106–107)
>
> I am a very foolish fond old man.
>
> (IV.vii.60)
>
> I am old and foolish.
>
> (IV.vii.85)

And he suggests, though never defines, a new concept of being loved in his reunion with Cordelia. But he never, in a single, summary speech, tries to put into words just what he has learned about himself. It is not Lear's method and it is not Shakespeare's. This is a play in which the questions are greater than the answers. In this respect it mirrors the imbalance of life itself, which keeps man always insecure—and in motion. If the big question had been fully, unmistakably answered, instead of powerfully raised and examined, and if Lear had finally left the stage as a fully rational and enlightened man instead of an exhausted, broken man in delirium, the play and the hero would have been of a different, inferior sort. This is not a didactic play and it is not an essay, with conclusion, in moral philosophy. Furthermore, Lear as an individual is too complex to have a single identity. His initial dignity and inflexibility make it easy to overlook his almost unsurpassed variety as a personality: his bitter wit, his sense of the dramatic—his clowning, engagingly and sentimentally pleading antics—along with his constantly recurring posture as Shakespeare's most regal monarch. He is also seen quite differently by different persons and by himself at different moments as he ranges in mood from arrogance, to rage, to self-pity, and to humble questioning; and these moods do not constitute a firm, irreversible progress. But I think that it is fair to regard his self-enlightenment—with the monumental exception of the enigmatic last scene—as dominated finally by the last of these moods.

There is, however, a better explanation for what might be called the limited explicitness of Lear's acknowledgment of his identity in a play that so insistently raises the question of this identity. As an unwilling student of himself, he is impelled by his own considerable intelligence, and by the precepts of the age in which he was created, to go well beyond himself in his quest for self-knowledge. A lesser character, born in a different era, would have found the answer to "Who is it that can tell me who I am?" in purely personal, temporary terms. His explicit answers would all have been to the effect that "I should not have resigned the kingdom," "I was an unwise father," or "I should have seen through the false love of Goneril and Regan." Lear's ultimate self-discovery is more universal and permanent than this. As a "philosopher," and a Renaissance one at that, he is content, in his self-study, with no answer short of the nature of man and of woman. In other words, "self" in his case connotes all of what it means to be a man.

Although I do not wish to overstress the possible relevance to *King Lear* of the Renaissance treatises on *nosce teipsum*, they do help us to explain why *any* Renaissance work dealing substantially with self-knowledge, whether it is a poem like Sir John Davies', a treatise like La Primaudaye's, or a play like *King Lear*, should sooner or later focus not upon man as a unique individual but upon the human condition in general. The play would do so, of course, not to the exclusion of the individual qualities of Lear as one man; but insofar as the play deals with self-knowledge, that self-knowledge would be at least partially concerned with what the Renaissance, as in the treatises, thought about man in general.

The substance of what these treatises say about man is well summarized by Lear's question "Is man no more than this?" Their procedure, it will be recalled, was to examine man through his unimpressive and vulnerable body, particularly as seen through his far from exalted needs, and to conclude that essential man was frail, unsophisticated, and corrupt. *King Lear* is of course not a mere dramatization of these treatises, and we have already seen ways in which Lear's quest for self-knowledge is not of an age but for all time. Even in this chapter, which is partially guided by the treatises, we shall not be able to match the drama fully with doctrine. Nevertheless, what Lear learns about himself is not too far removed from the precepts about man's condition and his needs as outlined in the treatises. Shakespeare simply has his own way, a very dramatic one, of phrasing and answering his question about man.

II
THE ART OF OUR NECESSITIES IS STRANGE

Lear's most profound insight into the contemptible stature of mere man is of course the "unaccommodated man" speech, provoked by the sight of the naked Edgar:

Is man no more than this? Consider him well. Thou ow'st the worm no silk, the beast no hide, the sheep no wool, the cat no perfume. Ha! here's three on's are sophisticated! Thou art the thing itself; unaccommodated man is no more but such a poor, bare, forked animal as thou art. Off, off, you lendings! come, unbutton here.

(III.iv.107–114)

In its concern with the superficial trappings that make the body of naked man "sophisticated," it is a part of the often studied "clothes theme" of the play.[1] It links with Lear's later:

[1] One of the best explanations of this theme is Thelma Greenfield's "The Clothing Motif in *King Lear*," *Shakespeare Quarterly*, V (1954), 281–286. An interesting extension of the clothing metaphor is suggested by Maynard

> *Through tatter'd clothes great vices do appear;*
> *Robes and furr'd gowns hide all.*
>
> (*IV.vi.168–169*)

Both speeches, however, proceed from and, in a sense, mark the conclusion to an essay whose major statement is the equally famous "O, reason not the need!" (II.iv.267), which is followed shortly by "The art of our necessities is strange . . ." (III.ii.70).

The point I wish to make is that Lear learns about unaccommodated man—his unwarranted pride and his frailty—through inquiring into man's necessities, which are in turn closely and humiliatingly related to his body. The "reason not the need" speech has too often been taken in isolation, as though it emerged suddenly from Lear's argument with his daughters about the necessary number of his retainers. I should like to show here how the subject pervades the play, becoming a part of Lear's self-discovery and leading him to a partial answer to the question "Is man no more than this?" For, if we "Allow not nature more than nature needs, / Man's life is cheap as beast's" (II.iv.269–270). A study of what "nature needs," of "the art of our necessities," begins in the first scene. And it begins in terms of Lear as an individual, gradually extending its dimensions to mankind.

Even when Lear announces his retirement, he is concerned, as is natural for the aged, with what will prove necessary. At first thought his intention seems to be a commendable one: he will "Unburden'd crawl toward death" (I.i.42). Already, in his first sizable statement, he is apparently reckoning what his needs as an old man will be. He wants merely enough so that he can "crawl" toward death. This is promising in its abject sense of man's ultimate stature; and in its wisdom about the humble pilgrimage of man's body it is a fitting complement to Lear's later "sermon":

> *When we are born, we cry that we are come*
> *To this great stage of fools.*
>
> (*IV.vi.186–187*)

Mack: "I suspect we are invited to sense, as Lear speaks, that this is a kingdom too deeply swaddled in forms of all kinds—too comfortable and secure in its 'robes and furr'd gowns'; . . ." *King Lear in Our Time* (Berkeley and Los Angeles: University of California Press, 1965), p. 94.

But a violent career of learning separates the two statements. The latter is deeply realized; the former is, in all probability, an unfelt recital thought to be suitable for the occasion.

It is clearly mistaken in respect to man's real needs. Its understanding of what old age needs spiritually, as opposed to its comforts, is shallow. "All cares and business" are disposed of as no longer necessary, when in fact, as Everyman and his early Renaissance stage kindred learn, the preparation for death must be attended by the most arduous of thoughtful concern. Again, there is only specious acceptance of man's final stage of crawling when Lear gives up "all the large effects / That troop with majesty" (I.i.133–134), for we recall that he is retaining "The name, and all th' addition to a king" (I.i.138). And, besides the false security and pomp that the name of king gives him, he is passionately insistent upon being attended, in what should be a lonely pilgrimage, by his hundred knights. These are precisely the type of "necessities" that cannot accompany Everyman in his final reckoning.

But though Lear will not impose a minimum existence upon himself, he promptly does so upon his two best and most devoted counselors, Cordelia and Kent. Cordelia is sent dowerless into the world, and Kent is allotted five days "for provision / To shield thee from disasters of the world" (I.i.176–177). (There is a strong adumbration of unaccommodated man in Lear's reference to Kent's "banish'd *trunk.*") The irony here is surely intentional. It prepares us to feel more powerfully Lear's own contact with the real experience of what "nature needs."

When we next see Lear, it is not as a man crawling toward death but as one returning from hunting. Perhaps we should not make too much of this form of retirement activity. But what stands out in this scene is that Lear's main concern is with his appetite. His first words are: "Let me not stay a jot for dinner; go get it ready" (I.iv.8–9). And a little later, he more querulously demands, "Dinner, ho, dinner!" (I.iv.46). This is a far cry from "Necessity's sharp pinch" (II.iv.214), which he will shortly vow to feel with the wolf and owl,[2] but it is an ironic foreglimpse of the

---

[2] He will also wander with "the belly-pinched wolf" (III.i.13).

later experience and emphasizes the shallowness of his earliest concept of minimum survival. Furthermore, he is beginning to feel, divested of the large effects that troop with majesty, the humiliating lesson of what his body will teach him.

The first real lesson in the subject of necessity which Lear will receive is partially noted in the preceding chapter. The Fool, one of whose main qualifications as tutor is his closeness to the problem of survival, schools Lear incessantly in the humblest needs of money, warmth, shelter, and labor. The Fool comments upon how "much the rent of his land comes to" (I.iv.147–148). He cites the lesson of the snail in having a house "to put 's head in; not to give it away to his daughters and leave his horns without a case" (I.v. 32–34). And his songs constantly emphasize the role that wealth has in human relationships. "Fathers that wear rags" are unregarded by their children. Fortune "Ne'er turns the key to th' poor" (II.iv.48–53). These snatches of basic learning ultimately strike home to Lear, though not fully until the storm scene. Then, when the Fool sings,

> "He that has and a little tiny wit,—
> With heigh-ho, the wind and the rain,—
> Must make content with his fortunes fit,
> For the rain it raineth every day,"
>
> (III.ii.74–77)

Lear makes one of his few clear signs of agreement: "True, boy." Here, the King is acknowledging both the modest necessities due to one who is foolish and the lesson in survival taught by the relentless elements.

It is, however, before the storm and in the quarrel scene with his two daughters at Gloucester's castle that affliction begins to give Lear real forebodings as to the true meaning of necessity and begins to enlarge his vision from his own importunate belly to the plight of mankind. There is probably more theatricality than real perception in his threat to Regan that rather than return to Goneril he will abjure all roofs and learn "Necessity's sharp pinch" (II.iv. 211–213). There is also theatricality in his dramatization of how he will kneel to Goneril and beg the necessities of life:

Age is unnecessary. On my knees I beg
That you'll vouchsafe me raiment, bed, and food.

(*II.iv.157–158*)

Nevertheless, these are the first generalized reflections upon necessity. They are motivated, of course, by his individual situation, by the apprehension that he is in fact almost homeless, and, most alarmingly, is himself "unnecessary." He has frantically hurried from Goneril's inhospitable castle to Gloucester's, where he has only grudgingly been allowed entrance. But he is also reaching, though it is mingled with self-pity and rage, that stage in his development as thinker when he can communicate with others. Beaten down by his daughters' cruel tightening of the bonds on what is symbolically so essential to him—the number of his retainers—and driven into helpless frustration by their coldly reasoned argument on what constitutes necessity in service,[3] he reacts with his "O, reason not the need!" speech.

This speech is more often quoted than analyzed, and indeed full explication is difficult because of Lear's rising hysteria. Nevertheless, we have seen it partly in a context that makes its emergence less remarkable. Lear has been learning about need even though he has not talked about it. Further, we can see that Lear is still not inclined, in any full sense, to accept a philosophy of man based upon only the essential needs. Lear would not reason the need because the conclusions are too unpleasant—are in fact exactly those he should have acknowledged as befitting a man crawling unburdened toward death: Even beggars lead a superfluous life; if we accept nature's definition of need, "Man's life is cheap as beast's"; nature does not need what a lady wears so gorgeously. Then, however, the discourse breaks off with:

But, for true need,—
You heavens, give me that patience, patience I need!
You see me here, you gods, a poor old man,
As full of grief as age; wretched in both!

(*II.iv.273–276*)

[3] For the concept of "service" in the play, see Jonas A. Barish and Marshall Waingrow, " 'Service' in *King Lear*," *Shakespeare Quarterly*, IX (1958), 347–355.

We shall never know exactly what Lear was going to say about "true need." Perhaps it is merely what he proceeds to say in self-pity. To him, at this point, true need is best exemplified by the heartrending spectacle he presents: old, wretched, rejected. But possibly too he is beginning, without yet a full awareness of what he seeks, to anticipate what he will learn about "poor naked wretches" in the storm scene.

Even without having seen any of these wretches, he is able under the tutelage of the storm and his own complaining body ("I am cold myself") to comment upon the plight, in terms of unmet needs, of the houseless thousands. Almost for the first time (if we except his solicitude for the shivering Fool), he goes beyond pity for himself to a vividly pictured awareness of what *man's* universal plight is:

> Poor naked wretches, wheresoe'er you are,
> That bide the pelting of this pitiless storm,
> How shall your houseless heads and unfed sides,
> Your loop'd and window'd raggedness, defend you
> From seasons such as these?
>
> (III.iv.28–32)

He admits that he has taken too little care of this and concludes with what may be one of the prominent purposes of the play's study of necessity:

> Take physic, pomp;
> Expose thyself to feel what wretches feel,
> That thou mayst shake the superflux to them
> And show the heavens more just.
>
> (III.iv.33–36)

Unquestionably the play is partly concerned with social justice and equitable distribution. This idea, so relevant to the theme of necessity, is reinforced by Gloucester's comparable insight that "the superfluous and lust-dieted man" should learn to feel so that "distribution should undo excess, / And each man have enough" (IV.i.70–74). But economic need and just distribution are, I think, only incidental to the play. More important is the lesson about the nature of man through his needs which will come when pomp takes physic and feels, through the body, what the simplest of men feel.

This lesson is dramatized by the entrance of Edgar as Poor Tom. It is naked, trembling Edgar who prompts Lear to his speech on unaccommodated man. And we should recall Edgar's earlier announcement of the nature and import of his disguise. He will

> *take the basest and most poorest shape*
> *That ever penury, in contempt of man,*
> *Brought near to beast.*
>
> (II.iii.7–9)

Later, too, Gloucester describes the disguised Edgar as one "Which made me think a man a worm" (IV.i.35).

Partly, then, through the sufferings of his own flesh and his reduction in status, partly by the spectacle of naked Edgar, and partly by the enlargement of his sympathy and vision, Lear gains a new insight into man through studying the art of our necessities. He finds it strange indeed. But he does finally, despite his eloquent protest, reason the need and find that man, stripped of his sophistication and "better in a grave," owes "the worm no silk, the beast no hide, the sheep no wool, the cat no perfume." Man, as a frail creature, is seen much in the manner of the Renaissance treatises. But that he is also a corrupt and tainted creature—that his "flesh and blood . . . is grown so vile"—we shall have to examine in a separate section.

To the present section, however, there must be added a further note that, for the sake of unity of theme, it would be better to omit. It would, in more ways than one, be convenient to disregard the final scene of the play. As Professor Harbage has said, "Each reader must come to terms with this ending in his own way, and with it he should prefer to be alone." [4] Besides its intimately

---

[4] Alfred Harbage, *William Shakespeare: A Reader's Guide* (New York: Noonday Press, 1963), p. 429. For one of the most painful explanations of the last scene, an explanation that makes one prefer to be alone with the play and not the interpretation, see J. Stampfer, "The Catharsis of *King Lear*," *Shakespeare Survey* 13 (1960), p. 10.

unique meaning to each reader, it is an enigmatic scene. Lear at the end is either irrational or suprarational. First carrying and then kneeling by the body of Cordelia, he is no longer the humbled man we last saw. He is now defiant and resentful. And it is in this mood that he makes his final comment upon the theme of necessity:

> No, no, no life!
> Why should a dog, a horse, a rat, have life,
> And thou no breath at all?
>
> (V.iii.305–307)

Man's life, he would now insist, is not as cheap as beast's. Unaccommodated man will not suffice him in this his worst ordeal of questioning. He demands a special status for man above the animals. Though he has gone through a brief career as philosopher, of the Montaigne persuasion, this philosophy will not sustain him through a personal tragedy. From his concern with man in general he pathetically returns—and this is one of the great dramatic touches of the play—to an overwhelming need for one person. Here, perhaps, we find the conclusion to his broken disquisition on "true need." There is no need like that of one individual for another. The aching need for Cordelia obliterates, as the loss of a loved one always does, all that philosophy has taught one. Naked man *is* "more than this."

III
ARE YOU OUR DAUGHTER?

Lear's education in the nature of man is of course not confined to the theme of "The art of our necessities." There are several insights, more or less separate from this theme, which help answer the question "Is man no more than this?" One thinks immediately of one of Lear's first recognitions that man is limited by his body. When Cornwall will not admit him, Lear breaks off his anger with the reflection that the Duke may not be well: "nature, being oppress'd, commands the mind / To suffer with the body" (II.iv.

109–110). A comparable, though reversed, relationship of mind and body is driven home personally and powerfully to Lear during the storm when he acknowledges that when the mind is free the body is delicate (III.iv.11–12). And, to take but one more example, he learns also from the storm the frailty and ineffectual quality of his kingly body. Wet by the rain and made to chatter by the wind, he "smelt" out his flatterers and learned that he was not "ague-proof" (IV.vi.102–107). The imagery of the lowly sense of smell, and what it here and elsewhere connotes in the play, reinforces the importance of the body in Lear's education and supports Mrs. Nowottny's fine perception: Shakespeare "has brought home to us Lear's belief that all a man can know is what he knows through the flesh." [5] But we must go beyond this statement. Lear not only learns through the flesh; he learns about the flesh and its limitations, its vileness. And this brings us to the substance of the present section, which is what Lear learns about man's, and his own, tainted body through woman.

Except for Cordelia, all references to women in the play are highly unpleasant.[6] *King Lear* is, in fact, so rank with the most revolting depictions of women and—even worse—woman, that it has been held, even by some conservative critics, to suggest the nadir of a period of sexual nausea through which Shakespeare himself was suffering. This conclusion has been generally based, for *King Lear* at least, upon the supposedly gratuitous nature of the sexual passages, by the manner in which they exceed dramatic and thematic requirements of the play. There seems to be little in the first part of the play to prepare for Lear's darkly clinical examination of a woman's body. He has not earlier, with one exception, used sexual imagery, and the vileness of sex seems to have little to do with either the reason for his tragedy or the nature of his ordeal. My explanation for Lear's sexual nausea is not meant to be

---

[5] "Lear's Questions," *Shakespeare Survey* 10 (1957), p. 92.

[6] For an argument that Shakespeare, despite all the unfavorable references to women in the play, did not intend *King Lear* as an indictment of sex, see Robert H. West, "Sex and Pessimism in *King Lear*," *Shakespeare Quarterly*, XI (1960), 55–60. Lear, according to West, is embittered against sexual generation mainly by unkind daughters.

exclusive of others.[7] All I have tried to do is explore the problem in the context of our subject, Lear's self-discovery, and perhaps in the context of its ultimate conclusion: "Is man no more than this?"

Man's naked body proved for Lear to be grimly instructive. But it stressed for him mainly what a pathetically grotesque creature man was. It did not make man seem revoltingly tainted in flesh. For the ultimate in Lear's discovery of man's naked condition Shakespeare turned to the body and appetites (as opposed to the needs) of woman. "Let them anatomize Regan" is then merely another stage in Lear's study of man's debased condition, but it is the final stage. Such a view makes less gratuitous the role of sex in the play. The anatomy of the female is not introduced because Shakespeare was sick—possibly not because Lear was sick—but in part because Lear was in his self-discovery investigating man's condition, and only woman's body could suffice to illustrate the full depravity of man.

But there is still another reason why we should not regard the theme of sex as an isolated and extradramatic aspect of Lear's characterization. It is placed in context. To appreciate how central it is to the play, we must know both that it is important to Lear's discovery of himself through man, and that the exposure of the sexuality of man (and woman) does not suddenly emerge in the mad scenes, but is in some ways prepared for earlier by other characters and by Lear's own actions and nature.

To Lear's education in the sexuality of woman, two other characters serve, very early in the play, as foils. Both Gloucester and Edmund have completed most of the curriculum, the latter with honors. In the twenty-fourth line of the play, Gloucester has learned that "the whoreson must be acknowledged." And we

[7] No layman, for example, should lightly rule out the Freudian view that analysis can never be accomplished without the most unpleasant surfacing of sex; and some of my conclusions are, I trust, not ignorant of Freud. But one may demur to this extent: Freud himself, with his Lear-like ability to shift his point of view even in old age, found the real issue in *King Lear* not to be sex but the acceptance of death. See "The Theme of the Three Caskets," in *Complete Psychological Works* (London: Hogarth Press, Ltd., 1958), XII, 289–301.

have already seen how he has become "braz'd" to his sexual life and remembers chiefly that "there was good sport at his making." Gloucester perhaps suffers as a result of his callous sensuality. Edgar later comments to Edmund:

> The dark and vicious place where thee he got
> Cost him his eyes.
>
> (V.iii.172–173)

But this recognition never comes to Gloucester himself. Unlike Lear, he never broods over man's mortality in terms of the "dark and vicious place." For all practical purposes within the play, Gloucester's education about sex is completed by the first scene.

Edmund's conception of the sexual element in man's nature is equally prompt and is more natively a part of his temperament. He suffers no disturbing disillusionment about the ideal nature of man and woman because he has never had any illusions. He is in this respect the perfect foil to Lear. Edmund is from the beginning happy with the "fierce quality" (I.ii.12) of sex. It is he who deplores the "evasion of whoremaster man, to lay his goatish disposition on the charge of a star" (I.ii.137–139), and he talks freely and happily about one of the subjects most painful for any sensitive youth (such as Hamlet) to contemplate: How "My father compounded with my mother" (I.ii.139–140).

For both Gloucester and Edmund the sexuality of life is fully, even gladly, conscious. With Lear it seems to be largely unconscious, but of course not absent. Lear's most shattering experience will be the answer to one of his many seemingly innocent questions: "Are you our daughter?" (I.iv.238). The final answer to this question will not be that the daughters are ungrateful, but that they are in the fullest physiological sense women. And not all of this discovery will come from any change in the behavior of the daughters; it will be the emergence of an aspect of himself which he had not known was there. He is discovering himself as well as his daughters. One does not have to subscribe to the theories of psychoanalysis to proceed from the premise that most of our knowledge is unconscious and that much of what we learn about others is in fact a disclosure of what is within us, unrecognized.

The first scene of the play, the "love scene," is a tempting one for the purpose of showing Lear's unacknowledged sexual attitudes. He is of course an extremely old man, and society—particularly its younger members like Hamlet—likes to think that old age, like infancy, is securely free from sexual needs or even interests. Shakespeare need not have been a modern, versed in the bookish theoric of psychoanalysis, to know that this is not so. This one play, in its sexual scenes, is ample proof of Shakespeare's "modern" awareness. Here we need take only one incidental passage, a kind of choral comment by the Fool: "Now a little fire in a wild field were like an old lecher's heart; a small spark, all the rest on's body cold" (III.iv.116–118).

Now Lear is not an old lecher; and the comment is not applied to him. But most of the Fool's remarks do have some point in the play as a whole, and one is justified in seeing them as at least choral. At any rate, some "small spark" *may* be present in Lear's anxious attitude toward his daughters' protestations of love. There *may* be latent incest, as there is in many men, in his wish for the unshared love of his daughters. Goneril and Regan verbally oblige, the latter even suggesting a sexual devotion in her avowal:

> . . . *I profess*
> *Myself an enemy to all other joys*
> *Which the most precious square of sense possesses.* . . .
>
> (I.i.74–76)

Although Kenneth Muir cites, in his Arden edition, several less disturbing (but not convincing) meanings of "the most precious square of sense," Neilson and Hill are probably right in glossing the expression as the "most exquisite region of my senses." Imagery such as this is not out of character for Regan as we later come to know her. It is she who will refer to "the forfended place" (V.i.11). However this may be, an expression of sexuality is not, as I shall presently argue, by any means what Lear wants to hear; but what would please him about the speech is the daughter's preference of his love for the pleasure a husband could give her. It is, however, Cordelia's response that he most needs, and so what angers him about it is that a daughter should be willing to share her love for him with a husband. Thence comes a part of Lear's resentment toward France, and his fantasying the successful suitor as "hot-blooded France" (II.iv.215). Latent feelings of incest could, therefore, possibly account for the violence of Lear's rejection of Cordelia: he himself has been rejected. But I am very doubtful about this explanation, which I have presented as sympathetically as possible.[8] I cite it, like the Regan image, only to show the possibility—badly needed to explain his subsequent outbursts —that Lear at the beginning of the play may be more concerned with sex than conventional critics (for whom furred gowns hide all) have recognized.

My own interpretation of Lear's desire in this scene—besides the need for identity through love—is I think based more closely on the text and is more compatible with the painfulness of Lear's self-discovery in terms of a sexual body. What Lear wants from the women in his life is their exclusive devotion to him shown in the form of solicitous cherishing. He gives a clue to what he has wanted, and to the reason why he has preferred Cordelia, when he says:

> *I lov'd her most, and thought to set my rest*
> *On her kind nursery.*
>
> *(I.i.125–126)*

Cordelia had signified for him, not sexuality, but comfort. As contrasted probably with her fierce, passionate sisters,

> *Her voice was ever soft,*
> *Gentle, and low; an excellent thing in woman.*
> *(V.iii.272–273)*

---

[8] It cannot, however, be dismissed as merely ridiculous or revolting. Incest became a serious, overt, and sympathetic subject in John Ford. Shakespeare had already deeply felt its morbid interest in *Hamlet*. For a technical examination of it in *King Lear*, see John Donnelly, "Incest, Ingratitude and Insanity: Aspects of the Psychopathology of *King Lear*," *Psychoanalytic Review*, XL (1953), 149–155; and Arpad Pauncz, "Psychopathology of Shakespeare's *King Lear*: Exemplification of the Lear Complex (A New Interpretation)," *American Imago*, IX (1952), 57–78.

And when Goneril has failed to give him his "kind nursery," he turns to her sister, "Who, I am sure, is kind and *comfortable*" (I.iv.328). Whereas Goneril's eyes "are fierce," Regan's "Do *comfort* and not burn" (II.iv.175–176). What Lear will above all resist, loathe, and fear in women is a sexuality that goes beyond the gentle.

There is of course no decisive sexual meaning in the brutal rejection of Lear by Goneril and Regan. The closest hint of it is in the perversion suggested by the daughters as flagellating mothers (ironically related to "kind nursery"). Goneril says:

> Now, by my life,
> Old fools are babes again, and must be us'd
> With checks as flatteries, when they are seen abus'd.
>
> (*I.iii.18–20*)

And once more there comes to mind the Fool's image of Lear, unbreeched, being spanked by his mother-daughters (I.iv.187–190). But this does not get into Lear's own imagery. His gradual disillusionment with his daughters is expressed, except for "Degenerate bastard!" (I.iv.275), mainly in terms of imagery of animals and of a diseased human body: "Detested kite!" (I.iv.284), "thy wolvish visage" (I.iv.330), "Most serpent-like" (II.iv.163), and

> a boil,
> A plague-sore, an embossed carbuncle,
> In my corrupted blood.
>
> (*II.iv.226–228*)

Although these images show that the daughters are becoming in his mind monsters of depravity, in a bodily sense, the responsibility for his shifting their vileness to sexual terms is Lear's own. He does not know of their lustful passion for Edmund (which at any rate comes later in the play).

He first becomes obsessed with Goneril as a breeder. This is partially understandable in view of her unkindness to the man who begot her. He would not have his unnatural daughter bear a child, and if she must have one, let the child be to her as she has been to him. What is not fully understandable is the violence and clinical precision of the curse in which he prays for Goneril's sterility. This anatomizing of Goneril comes, it should be remembered, early in the play. It is the first sustained expression of his outrage against his daughter, and it is significant that his early revulsion against an act of ingratitude should be concerned primarily with "the organs of increase" and "her derogate body." This early concern at any rate makes less extraneous his final and repellent anatomy of the female in Act IV.

What I think it shows mainly is that the "filth" of the sexuality is partly within Lear himself. The imagery of the play as a whole would support the interpretation of a vile imagination projecting its own image on the world, and of concealed vileness breaking from its bounds and disclosing itself. In his mad speech on sex, Lear himself attributes it to his imagination: "good apothecary, sweeten my imagination" (IV.vi.132–133). But other passages in the play are equally illuminating. Lear speaks of "Close pent-up guilts" riving their "concealing continents" (III.ii.57–58). Cordelia also stresses the idea that filth will disclose itself (as it does in the way she predicts): "Who covers faults, at last shame them derides" (I.i.284). And Albany points perhaps most explicitly of all to the source of foul imaginations: "Filths savour but themselves" (IV.ii.39). Lear is, then, in a manner both dramatically and psychologically convincing, discovering—though at first it is more exposing than discovering—some unsavory truths about himself. He is revolted and yet fascinated by the sexual female, as opposed to the kind whose voice is ever soft, gentle, and low.

What, however, is the agent that brings about this exposure? If he were mad, like Ophelia, it would be understandable. But he is still sane. He is, to be sure, in his rising hysteria moving toward madness. It is only a little more than a hundred lines later that he cries:

> O, let me not be mad, not mad, sweet heaven!
> Keep me in temper; I would not be mad!
>
> (I.v.50–51)

But it should be stressed that the curse, unlike his later anatomy of woman, is, though intense, cruelly controlled.[9] The sexual imagery is even here close enough to the surface to emerge without madness. It is, then, a fairly conscious part of his growing awareness of sexuality and the horror of the corrupt female body.

And what increases the horror for him, and also shows his early interest in the female body, is that these monsters are seemingly fair creatures. He twice emphasizes their youth and beauty. The child of spleen is to stamp wrinkles in Goneril's "brow of youth." The fen-sucked fogs are to "infect her beauty" (II.iv.168). And they have the outward form of woman ("Thou art a lady," "gorgeous" in dress), which makes their vileness all the more terrible, even as man's furred gowns enhance the guilt that they conceal. Albany later expresses what is doubtless Lear's far more intense disillusionment:

> *Proper deformity seems not in the fiend*
> *So horrid as in woman.*
>
> (*IV.ii.60–61*)

Lear's own steps in the way of sexual discovery are, as we note in the preceding chapter, materially assisted by the Fool, whose imagery and songs are full of references to sex and to the sexual nature of both men and women. Here again one is tempted to see the Fool as a part of Lear himself. Another catalyst is Poor Tom, who (like the Fool appearing only when Lear is ready for his lesson) not only teaches Lear about unaccommodated man, but helps him, through provocative suggestion, to fantasy genteel ladies seducing curly-headed servingmen to sate their lust. "Let not," he cautions further, "the creaking of shoes nor the rustling of silks betray thy poor heart to woman. Keep thy foot out of brothels, thy hand out of plackets . . ." (II.iv.97–100).

But despite these catalysts, it is Lear's own imagination that is

---

[9] Harley Granville-Barker writes of this curse: "The actor who will rail and rant this famous passage may know his own barnstorming business, but he is no interpreter of Shakespeare. The merely superficial effect of its deadlier quiet, lodged between two whirlwinds of Lear's fury, should be obvious." *Prefaces to Shakespeare*, First Series (London: Sidgwick & Jackson, Ltd., 1949), p. 169.

responsible for his ultimate anatomy of woman in Act IV. Early references to female sexuality have partially, but not fully, prepared us for this savage outburst. And doubtless if we had been prepared for it, it would have been, as would Ophelia's sex in madness, far less dramatic.

I need not run through all the details of Lear's speech on the anatomy of woman beneath the waist. This is more painful to the senses than the scene of the blinding of Gloucester, for, unlike stage business, imagery cannot be wholly or partly concealed. I suspect, of course, that this speech is usually not "explicated" in college classrooms. This is understandable. I would emphasize, however, that the speech is not pornography; it is philosophy. There is a profound distinction that separates sex in this play from the bawdy of the comedies.[10] Curiously, *King Lear* is Shakespeare's only tragedy that is, like the happy comedies, a play of "generation." But whereas talk of generation in the comedies takes the spirited, lighthearted, and expectant form of bawdy, in *King Lear* it is humorless, unprovocative, and pessimistic. In the comedies, generation stands for the joyous vitality and renewal of life, the future of all that the courtship plots are about. In *King Lear*, generation not only breeds monstrous children; it points toward mortality and sin. It is finally not an agent of renewal, but a fantasy in the mind of a man near death. Critics and teachers who scant Lear's anatomy of woman have the doubtful virtue, then, of silencing not prurience but philosophy. They miss the important aspect of generation in "we came crying hither" (really the tragic sequel to the gay courtship of the comedies), and they miss what Shakespeare's contemporaries may well have considered the play's deepest and darkest view of the nature of man.

What I should like to stress further about the speech, besides its comment upon man, is why the fantasy is the most painful one that Lear could conjure up for himself. For Lear the painful part of the image is not just the horror of "the sulphurous pit," but the fact that this is a usually disguised part of seemingly gentle

---

[10] It is significant that even so vigilant a student of bawdy as Eric Partridge apparently does not see fit to mention Lear's anatomy speech. *Shakespeare's Bawdy* (London: Routledge & Kegan Paul, 1955).

woman. What revolts him—and this goes back to his preference
for the mild Cordelia—is the exposed sexuality of

> yond simp'ring dame,
> Whose face between her forks presages snow,
> That minces virtue, and does shake the head
> To hear of pleasure's name. . . .
>
> (*IV.vi.120–123*)

As with man, Lear has now anatomized woman, and he has
done so "down from the waist." In both instances, what repels
him is the nakedness beneath the sophistication. As the Renaissance treatises recommended, he had discovered part of himself
through unaccommodated man. But with woman he reaches one
step further and sees not just the weakness but the vileness of humanity. It is perhaps this that leads him, when Gloucester asks to
kiss his hand after the speech about woman, to say: "Let me wipe
it first; it smells of mortality" (IV.vi.136).

It may be objected that, because Lear is mad in this scene, he
achieves little valid self-discovery. Actually, however, it is not, as
we have seen, the complete lack of reason found in Ophelia's
exhibitionism. It is more accurately described by Edgar as "reason
in madness" (IV.vi.179). Moreover, earlier in the play, while he
was still sane, Lear had reached a recognition of his own share in
his daughters' vileness, a recognition that in part is merely fulfilled
by his fantasy concerning woman during his madness. The "reasonable" part of his perception during Act IV—amplified to be
sure by a powerful projection through his imagination—is that his
daughters are but extensions of himself. He had told Goneril:

> . . . yet thou art my flesh, my blood, my daughter;
> Or rather a disease that's in my flesh. . . .
>
> (*II.iv.224–225*)

And, a little later, when he is verging on madness, he had been
able to recognize that

> 'Twas this flesh begot
> Those pelican daughters.
>
> (*III.iv.76–77*)

To at least this extent, therefore, he has sanely participated in his final anatomy of woman. And for our purposes he has made an equally important step toward self-discovery, for he has not simply externalized the vileness in some form apart from himself.

But, as at the end of the last section, we must again face the fact that Lear's mad scene does not conclude the play. Having been through this purgatory of self-discovery, he returns to full sanity momentarily and before his final defiance becomes a humble, relatively tranquil man, his "rage" gone. Once more he wants, it would seem, to retire to Cordelia's "kind nursery" when the two are taken to prison. This is dramatically, but not philosophically, a logical outcome of the pilgrimage he has been through. He cannot sustain indefinitely the intensity of his vision. His spiritual pilgrimage, unparalleled in Shakespeare elsewhere, has been accomplished so far as an old man, and so far as Shakespeare looking through an old man's eyes, could accomplish it. There was no more in this tough world for him to learn. What remained was, in Webster's words, "another voyage."

Index

Index

Abasement of the Proud King, 100;
and Lear, 100, 101

Abernethy, John
*Christian and Heavenly Treatise,
Containing Physicke for the
Soule, A*, 16, 18, 21 n. 9, 24, 25

Achievement of self-knowledge: Lear
and, 3–4, 6, 7, 115–116, 134–
135; difficulty of, 16–18, 35;
Angelo's, 27–28; Richard II's
lack of, 51; Brutus' lack of, 58–
59; Edgar's, 88

Adam, 21, 26, 30, 106

Adams, Robert P.
"King Lear's Revenges," 97 n. 4

Admonitions to self-knowledge, 15–
16; and *King Lear* audience, 15

Affliction: as guide to self-knowledge,
18–20, 35; lessons of, 19; and
Lear, 35; of body vs. mind in
King Lear, 35; of Richard III,
48; storm and, 72; necessity and
Lear's, 120

Alarbus (*Titus Andronicus*), 47

Albany, Duke of (*King Lear*), 69
n. 12, 85, 86, 131, 132

Alienation. *See* Displacement, man's
sense of

Allegorical criticism. *See* Christian interpretations

Alma (*The Faerie Queene*), 42

Anagnorisis. *See* Aristotle

"Anatomy of Angst, The," 101

Angelo (*Measure for Measure*): and
acknowledgment of own nature
and errors, 3, 28; self-recognition
of, as man, 26–28; self-discovery
of Lear and, 27; and "feeling
sense" of own deformities, 27–
28; sex in, 28

Anger: grief and, 37–39; danger of

smothering, 38; Shakespeare's
awareness of grief as, 38; and
grief in Hamlet, 38, 39; Lear's
conversion of grief to, 38–39

Angst, 100–101

Animals: man and, 25–26; and "beast
theme" in *King Lear*, 25–26;
imagery of, 130

Answers vs. questions in *King Lear*,
115

Antony, Mark (*Julius Caesar*), 3, 7,
56–57, 59

Apologie for Poetrie, An. See Sidney,
Sir Philip

Appetite, minimum survival and
Lear's, 119–120

Archetypal basis for Lear, 100–101

Argument: of Lear and daughters, 37,
74–75, 102, 121; and Tarquin's
self-debate vs. self-inquiry, 45; absence of, in Titus, 47; and self-
debate in Richard III, 50; and
self-debate in Brutus and Claudius, 50; and absence of self-debate in Lear, 50; and self-debate
in Hamlet, 50, 65; and Richard
II, 51–52; in Brutus, 56; in Lear,
70, 74–76, 95, 102; Lear's lack
of preparation for, 75; and depiction of Lear's thought, 76; co-
herence of Lear's, 76; of Lear
and wills of heavens, 92. *See also*
Conversation; Thinking; Thinking in Lear

Aristotle, 12 n. 1; and anagnorisis, 2–
4; Shakespeare's acquaintance
with *Poetics* of, 2, 4; on recognition as essential of great tragedy,
2, 3–4; recognition and audience,
2, 3; peripeteia, 3; and Lear's
recognition, 3–4

DATE DUE